£9-95

£1·99

30/2

CW00952196

My Kleinian Home

A Journey through
Four Psychotherapies

N I N I H E R M A N

'an association in which the free development of each
is the condition of the free development of all'

Free Association Books / London / 1988

Published 1988 by
Free Association Books
26 Freegrove Road
London N7 9RQ

First published by Quartet Books Limited 1985

Copyright © 1985 by Nini Herman
Postscript copyright © 1988 by Nini Herman
Illustrations and drawings copyright © 1985 by Josef Herman

British Library Cataloguing in Publication Data

Herman, Nini
My Kleinian home.
1. Psychoanalysis. Herman, Nini
I. Title
150.19'5'0924
ISBN 1-85343-049-8

Typeset by AKM Associates (UK) Ltd, Southall, London
Printed and bound in Great Britain

For my children, for Josef and Dr K

Contents

Acknowledgements

I would like to acknowledge with warmest thanks the encouragement and suggestions generously offered by Harold Bourne, Rosemary Draper, Robert Hinshelwood, Levane Marshall, Donald Meltzer, Jan and Dan Miller, Hanna Segal, Gerald Wooster, and the late Mrs Ilse Seglow and to express my gratitude to Josef and the children for their continuous support.

The poem 'Ithaka' by C.P. Cavafy, translated by Rae Dalvin, is reproduced by kind permission of Chatto & Windus Ltd.

Have Ithaka always in your mind.
Your arrival there is what you are destined for.
But don't in the least hurry the journey.
Better it last for years,
So that when you reach the island you are old,
Rich with all you have gained on the way,
Not expecting Ithaka to give you wealth.
Ithaka gave you the splendid journey.
Without her you would not have set out.
She hasn't anything else to give you.
And if you find her poor, Ithaka hasn't deceived you.
So wise have you become of such experience,
That already you'll have understood what these Ithakas mean.

C. P. Cavafy: Ithaka.

Introduction

We are conceived and we are born. Looked at in this simple way each of us begins life twice. But mankind has always held, with ceremonial ritual, that a third and later birth is the one which really counts. One is then, we say today, born psychologically.

What exactly does this mean? What process of development leads towards this later birth long after life inside the womb has been exchanged for life outside? We all know that a baby smiles; learns to support his head; sits up; begins to crawl and then to walk. These are the landmarks we can see and delight in day by day without any special skill. Yet there are others which we may not be able to observe except, perhaps, in retrospect, and which can only be deduced by observers in this recent field. It was slowly opened up as the work begun by Freud was extended to explore the human mind from the very hour of birth and even prior to that event.

What is the nature of this learning which proceeds in the dark during the first months of life and long before a baby talks? It is to distinguish, first of all, what is him from what is mother; but before he gets to that whole person who is mother, to separate mouth from breast, what is tongue from what is nipple. To learn the difference between what is inside and what is outside – both of mother and himself – between the 'me' and the 'not me' which will, in time, become the other: a basic geography without which there will be confusion which will interfere with later learning.

This process will go hand in hand with learning about love and hate, with the great discovery that the frustrating, absent mother is, incredibly, the same as she who comes and feeds and soothes away the fear of dying; whose presence makes the world outside a friendlier and safer place and not so dismal an exchange for the cosy antechamber where everything ran nice and smoothly, where

1

that purring powerhouse, the placenta, was in charge, and where mother's heartbeat reached us faintly through a murmuring sea.

Once this basic ABC has been established, development can go ahead. Without it, difficulties lie in store which may later prove beyond our powers to correct. For if, at its inception, the forward drive encounters such fundamental obstacles, it will begin to twist and turn. Instead of a trusting give and take, life becomes a strategy whose very terrors are denied. Such a child will not be ready to be born presently as a separate entity with its own distinctive boundaries. He or she will tend to back-track in significant respects, even if intelligence, or some other special gifts permit of spurious success.

This is the story of a child trapped in such dilemmas for virtually five decades, prevented during all this time from enjoying access to her true potentialities. It tells of the attempts she made over a quarter of a century to seek remedy, and is her way of offering thanks that those who helped her finally possessed the patience, love and skill to pick the scattered pieces up, clean and then assemble them into a person who was whole. How far the end result approximates to the intention at the starting post is something I shall never know but it feels sound and safe and true: have we the right to ask for more? Moreover such an undertaking is truly difficult to share. Nor is the reason hard to find. It lies enmeshed in the guilt and shame of discovering that we are not as we like to think we are, or insist we ought to be.

When Freud first told us that, from birth, we were assertive combatants manoeuvring to satisfy progressive claims of satisfaction and not simply pretty articles, we showered abuse upon his head. And when, within a few decades, Melanie Klein pursued the same path, revealing that the infant's mind, far from proverbial innocence, is from the very first a stage on which hate and love and death and life must fight it out with tooth and claw, we started hounding her as well. Thus do we avidly overturn the cornerstones of Natural Law, fully determined to save face within our web of make believe.

The help I sought eventually arrived by the oldest route such salvage operations take: that of one individual's true concern for another in distress. In our lifetime one of these routes is called psychoanalysis. At its heart lies, half asleep, the age-old revelation that man is a stranger to himself, to his deepest motives and to his inner, psychic life.

What *is* psychoanalysis? And how precisely does it work? This is not a textbook but a very personal account. It is set out in the belief that every true experience must reach out to others, like ourselves, since our inner universe is essentially of a piece. Were this not so, man's future would appear even more bleak than we see it in our day. And so I need not theorize but let the tale speak for itself.

But if we cut this Gordian knot of theoretical debate so blithely, it can still be said that psychoanalysis brings about a transformation which will lead gradually towards that birth which has at some point been postponed. And that no matter how unique every analysis may be, it will commonly begin with mental stasis and chaos. Upon this archaic mix the analytic yeast will begin, very gradually, to work. Although I was a doctor myself when my treatment first began, chaos was my starting point; for neither status nor position are guarantees of sanity.

It was another's chaos, however, that sprung the trap through which this book found the freedom to emerge. It was her total, maddening chaos, impinging on the remnants of my own, that crystallized a shaft of light in the asylum where I worked. For Cynthia (which is not her real name) obliged me one day to confront the patients I was treating then as someone who, just like themselves, had failed the people I loved the most. This painful moment is described in the first chapter, which bears Cynthia's name. From it I drew the courage to confront a wider readership. There is no data, I believe, that we have the right or reason to withhold, whatever the conventions claim, if are others who may come to utilize it in their way. For every true experience adds to that archipelago from which ripples ultimately spread out towards the wider shores that thirst for comradeship and love.

During the writing of this book I came to hear that Cynthia had died. She drowned off the Greek coast near Athens where with Yanos, whom she loved, she ran a refuge for lost dogs, with all of the significance that this touching choice implies. Of her death Yanos said, 'She simply dived into the waves and just did not come up again – good, strong swimmer that she was.' She had rejected help and care. Like so many others, she gave the quest up far too soon. All too frequently they choose a living or an actual death, rather than run the risk of being reached and freed and known. After this 'In Memoriam' the tale unfolds in straight chronology. In the beginning was my mother. At the end was Dr K. In between, my Jungian mother, Freudian father and a short therapeutic interlude. When I started on the book I had not discovered yet that I owed to each of them an equal debt of gratitude. Today, what then seemed like five steps has become a unity, the foundation of my life. Those whose lives have never passed through these tortuous corridors may ask in anger or dismay what all the fuss is about: to ensure that we are born as a separate entity is one of our basic rights. Without that struggle we may never flower to our full potential and give our best in work and love.

Cynthia

How often I heard the name from G, who is my second child.

'Nini, I am going to Israel with Cynthia.'

'Nini, I am going to Scotland, to stay with Cynthia in Dundee.'

'Nini, listen, Cynthia is in a mental hospital again.' There is, as matters stand with G, always someone in her life whose name falls on my inner ear with that invasive urgency ambulance sirens instil, or some unanswered telephone pleading in an endless night. At that time it was Cynthia's name. The name is sometimes of a girl; at others it can be a boy. The two seem interchangeable as I listen to the wavering sound, plangent with contagious fear that such a trophy must get lost, a dreadful and recurring fate that one seems helpless to avert.

This is how G, my daughter, feels. Only, like myself in former times, she must deny this constant, underlying fear that no one loves her, nobody will stay. And so it finds expression in a never-ending search; a frenetic restlessness.

Yet nothing seemed remarkable on the first evening we met. A shy girl, Cynthia focused on her postgraduate studies in South American literature and all her solitary trips through those far regions of the world, in an unobtrusive voice that often faded, like a dream. Her very nearly pretty face jarred like a jigsaw puzzle that has not been assembled quite right, however difficult to put a finger on the actual place. The eyes were clear and very blue, the colour of forget-me-nots. The fine hair, wavy and quite fair, reached to shoulders whose stoop suggested that something heavy must have rested there far too soon, though probably it was the mouth that was out of keeping with the rest. Looking at the mouth alone one would have thought the person cried, or spoke in anger or contempt. And looking back on that first meeting now,

5

uneventful as it seemed, it is clear that she was pleading, in the oldest language of mankind: 'Are you the one to take me in and save me from this painful fate of standing on my own two feet; from this world of degrees and more degrees I had to set up for myself to avoid adult responsibility which is the thing that scares me most, though I may not admit the fact to you or even to myself. Save me, because I know I can't go on much longer at this pace, trapped in this unreality and with no ground beneath my weary feet, no substance in my inner heart, the nothingness prevailing there.'

I knew that language from my past. I had confirmed it in my work. But I was tired and obtuse before a badly-needed summer holiday. And so I failed to recognize I had been urgently addressed, in Martin Buber's moving sense of the word, and lost the opportunity to enter into dialogue. Then summer ended. The young people returned from their islands and their summer haunts. Student flights shuttled them back to English soil, seemingly healthy and restored. Again the name of Cynthia wailed at ever shorter intervals over my evening telephone. G and Cynthia shared a room in Kilburn. It was wonderful. G and Cynthia shared a room in Cambridge. It was beautiful. Cynthia and G were full of schemes. New courses and a PhD. 'Smashing' was the word, I think, with its euphoric undertones, brittle and bright as plastic gold.

One day there came a change of plans. G was going to come back and work in London where the money was better than in the provinces. But she would naturally spend weekends in Cambridge with her friend. They'd be together in their room and it would be just marvellous. London was really such a dump. Who'd want to spend their weekends there? Then came an opportunity to visit them and see the room. Cambridge had been so beautiful that luminous October day. Bathed in sunlight after rain, the place glowed honey-gold and green like a medieval tapestry, a city of eternal dreams, as we strolled along the 'backs' with D and several of his friends – a generation of new freshmen drunk on open-handed promises of life.

After a day such as that the room came as a grievous shock. In a hapless, dingy letting house cowering in a treeless street floundered this ill-lit ground-floor room. G was crouching on the floor, inches from a tiny fire, leafing through a paperback, waiting for us to scoop her up and back to London for another week. Cynthia, clearly quite distraught, flurried around her like a moth.

Had she her handkerchief and pen? Her stockings, money and her purse? Her key for London and a cardigan? Would B, our youngest, maybe like some bread and treacle? Or perhaps some milk? Cynthia procured these instantly. It seemed a matter of first aid. Did I want bread and treacle too?

Something quite despairing broke through this bid to succour us. The poor girl felt that life itself was lost with G's departure now. The room was breaking with this pain of Cynthia, who would be alone, abandoned for five days and nights yet was unable to express the desolation of her rage, unable to confront her tears, her sense of utter helplessness. The others now seemed all at once in a great rush to get away. It seemed I was the only one aware of what was going on.

But there was nothing I could do. I knew the language and I knew the signs. For I myself had once been like that, adrift on the wild seas of life, without a compass or a flare, swept ever nearer to the brink. But there was nothing I could do since nobody had asked for help; yet I knew the call was bound to come urgent with emergency.

Then, sure enough, G telephoned within a matter of days. Wasn't it time, she probed, we met. There was this nice Greek eating place, a stone's throw from the Harrow Road. Could we not meet there for a meal? Now! In half an hour's time. Her voice gave nothing much away and yet I felt electrified by a panic that had not been voiced and for that very reason struck more deeply and relentlessly. That night G looked desperate and distraught. Neither the appetizing food nor the bouzoukis, nor the wine could dispel her simmering distress. Cynthia had broken down again. Their Cambridge landlady had rung to say that she was weeping all the time, banging her head against the wall and absolutely not herself. She had been housebound all week and not gone to the library once, as was her habit other days. And G was shaking; what was she supposed to do with this reversal of their roles? Now Cynthia was the helpless child and G was wholly unprepared to meet such a contingency. What should be done and what made

Cynthia act like that and why did she keep breaking down and how would I put Cynthia right and would it take me many days, G probed with desperation, hoping for a magic wand. Meanwhile I saw my image of the girl, those dislocated jigsaw parts that were the merest surface signs of serious fractures deep within. And from the little that I knew I guessed that every time G left, Cynthia concluded from this simple fact that all the good and loving things she kept on heaping on her friend with such compulsion were patently not good enough; for if they were why would G leave?

These matters I could understand since I had been like Cynthia once and had discovered in my own analysis that to the very insecure, the countless Cynthias of this world, every separation means total rejection, nothing less. The confirmation of a lifelong fear that one is never good enough, never deserving of another's love. The proof is that they go away. They go away, this logic runs in vicious circles all its own, because one is not good enough, clever or thoughtful or kind enough and so falls short of some ideal that one imagines must exist. And if one has not found it then it must come with the next friend, or lover as the case may be. And when it fails to turn up there, the fragile and the insecure are ejected once again into the hell-fire of their hate with all its destructive fantasies. The damage subsequently done is irreparable in fantasy. The world and those they need the most are felt to be in smithereens, or even worse, the terror runs, may presently retaliate. This mobilizes crushing guilt and devastating self-reproach, a common sequence of events the psychiatric textbooks still refer to as 'endogenous depression'. This means depression without cause, which the pundits treat with ECT or a variety of pills.

I knew that Cynthia had been through several such episodes in several mental hospitals; a wretched fate for one so young. The question at this moment was did she herself now have a wish, indeed a real priority, to get to grips with it all. I knew from my experience that resoluteness in these things is slow to ripen, frequently, nevertheless I said to G that I would see Cynthia, provided that she wanted help and was not merely playing games.

The evening Cynthia came along she looked just like her voice had sounded on the telephone that day: full of self-hatred and despair.

Clearly a dreadful anger that could not possibly be faced seethed in some compartment of her mind. As the story of her life slowly unfolded through her tears, I first pricked up my inner ear on hearing that at the age of twelve Cynthia had begged and pleaded to be sent away to boarding school, although none of her siblings went and it was not in any way traditional in her family. Nor was I then surprised to hear that things there went rather awry in various perplexing ways. For instance, some compulsion had made her burn the midnight oil, studying through half the night under her blankets with a torch, in some great frenzy to excel. And therefore I could ask myself if perhaps the anxieties of not accomplishing the break from home, or of having to be perfect, might have urged her upon this course that her parents had dismissed as a whim or headstrong choice.

Leaving such thoughts to one side, I heard that she had nonetheless got into university. There everything seemed relatively fine until, on a 'sandwich' course in Paris, and further from home than she had ever been, Cynthia broke down for the first time. Studying Existential thought in self-imposed solitude, the despairing undertones of those austere themes awoke such echoes in herself that it became more than she could bear. Apathetic and depressed, she was repatriated and admitted to a mental hospital where she underwent ECT. The vicious circle had begun.

If I myself had only gradually come to understand these things through my own experience, Cynthia in the here and now was far from understanding them. For there she was and there she sat, tearful, dishevelled from her flight from some pursuing inner rage, searching wildly through her scrapheap for some identity or clue or rhyme or reason as to who she was or who her nearest were, whom she should turn to in her plight, whom she should care for, or repair – while she was totally oblivious to the paradox all this implied.

Helpless and dazed, she felt compelled to reassure me endlessly that she needed neither food nor drink nor anything from me at all; yet every time I left the room she snatched an apple or a cake. Or she would gulp down all the milk, only to weep that now we had none left for breakfast when tomorrow came. Like me, when my analysis began, she had to deny her simplest needs in her terror that acknowledgement would make them endless in her eyes. But even if I understood something of these deeper things, at that late hour, in every sense, it was a case of first things first. And so I asked if she would like to come into my hospital, not into a conventional ward, but to the unit where I worked – a psycho-therapeutic community for young people like herself. I said it was the best thing I knew for someone in her predicament.

Cynthia dithered. She would have to go and think it over, even though she was in no state to think. G naturally felt the same. For now I was 'the enemy', because I had not come up with the hoped-for magic wand. Besides, was I not going to separate her from her friend out of malice or maternal spite? And so I had to let them go and face the difficult and lonely task of keeping human boundaries in repair, accepting sadly that for the time-being anyway I had done everything a mortal can who helps another to mobilize a sense of his autonomy. For to trespass in that domain, whatever pretext we deploy, will sooner or later undermine that tentative first burgeoning.

So several anxious days dragged by before the two declared defeat. 'OK, you win,' the message raged, but G was 'going to take her in'. And I, who had so far abstained from making any conditions instantly fell for theirs, only recognizing far too late that I had blundered desperately. I had walked straight into the trap set by my own unconscious guilt where certain areas of my life still lay enshrouded in my fear of pain, areas concerned with the overwhelming grief that I had abandoned G as a little child.

And so the stage was set for doom at my own initiative. Nor were difficulties slow to manifest themselves. Already on the following day, after Cynthia had arrived and G had helped her to settle in, the group which I ran three times a week talked in riddles. This was nothing very new; the patients in that Unit were for the most part young and quite disturbed, significantly out of touch with their feelings and experience. But on that morning what they said and what remained unsaid seemed unusually obscure. Gradually it dawned on me that the subject matter was pointing to certain things it was safer not to know.

At first I felt the theme was sex, but this solution did not seem to make deeper sense. At last the answer struggled through my own repression and the rampant fears that this 'material' provoked, with torrents of anxiety. G had been here. Yes, of course. The thing one must not know about was obviously connected with mothers and daughters, nothing less. And sure enough, that intervention shed instant daylight on the murky scene. G had spread the word around the previous evening to one and all, that I had not looked after her since the age of three or four. And she had added as an afterthought that she and I of course now lived 'absolutely separate lives' and that she didn't 'give a damn'.

'Isn't that wonderful,' gushed Ann, 'that's what we all want, isn't it, to be able to live separate lives!'

She beamed and waited for applause.

My impulse was to leave the room and blast G down the telephone. But that was hardly feasible. With no choice other than to sit tight in that very lonely chair, unable to act out the rage I knew was once more protecting me, I felt as if the information had tumbled into my ownership for the first time in my life . . . that I had not been with my child, my daughter G, since she was four! This, at a moment when I had to keep my wits about me, come what may, through a long morning of demanding work. My session in my Kleinian home, in the early afternoon, seemed a thousand years away.

'When I heard it,' Ann went on, 'I thought that Dr Herman must have been so jolly busy with her lovely work, when her little girl was four. That's what her daughter really meant. Her daughter's super, isn't she? So enthusiastic and beautifully cared for, obviously. I mean, well, anyone can see.'

Under the tremendous strain Ann's defences of total denial were operating once again. And although after three long years of work she had improved to the extent that she was no longer compelled to idealize me *quite* so much, uncontainable anxieties nevertheless made her return to earlier modes of defensiveness against a dangerous 'no-good' and hence 'cruel' inner mother of her own. For this she needed endless reassurances that I was perfect and could never do anything less than perfect in the course of my life. And other members of the group were in a comparably leaky boat, although to varying degrees. Though I rather hoped that one or two were by this time just strong enough to help me with the task of facing what must be faced. And as that morning's group at last ground to its ninety minutes' end on this half-mad, euphoric note,

I knew that Ann had just handed me the perfect conspiracy for getting off that awful hook.

Certainly, in former times, I would have grabbed at it urgently because I would have been compelled to save my precious self-image at any narcissistic price, even at the cost of undoing some of the good work we had accomplished through the patient years. But that was in the past. If formerly I would have been convinced, on the strength of my bleak, fragmented inner world, that this was the only bolt-hole left, if two decades ago I still assumed that I had nothing truly good to offer to my two small girls, there was a different 'I' by now, rooted in my Kleinian home. But if I had this haven now, fostering my sanity and slowly growing self-belief and trust in everything I had to give, my duties as a consequence were more far-reaching this time round. And so upon the following day, when the group met again, Ann's denial had to be taken up and scrutinized. Mustering every ounce of love and sense we shared between us in that shaky room, we had now steadfastly to face the rapids of anxiety: if the 'mother' therapist proves fallible in any way, the rage and let-down and despair might leave no option other than to destroy her totally. And this we had to look at now, sooner than the group's own needs and maturity required. Certainly sooner than I myself felt ready to confront the task, before inspecting my own wounds.

It proved tough going for the group. Its newest member, 'Little Nell', as ill as Ann had been years ago, fell fast asleep in self-defence. Molly lit endless cigarettes, although she had been cutting down. Ann kept running for cold drinks, Peter to relieve himself. Everyone had to resort, all of a sudden, once again, to some magical resource, as in the first months of the group, seeing that this 'food', myself, was under question now. Gradually, step by step – that day was just the start of it – we had to face the fact that psychotherapists are human beings who may also have difficulties and perhaps, even great sorrows of their own; that very often they themselves have faltered too, and made mistakes of far-reaching significance, such as failing people whom they love. To you, this may seem nothing new. But to the faltering and very frail, those who require long, intensive care and the very basic nurturing which goes by the name of psychotherapy, ideas like this can prove explosive stuff that may blow everything achieved apart or clear the ground for further growth.

I knew without a trace of doubt that the outcome in those anxious days depended on my steadfastness and my willingness to deal my precious self-image any blow, provided I did not undo the trust my patients might one day hopefully repose in me. I think we made it in the end. I think we returned from those dark seas together. My colleagues stood firm and supportive at my side. I had felt able to share my thoughtlessness with them and we were a close-knit, tolerant team, under good consultantship. Even so, I could not have solicited help like this, even a short time before, nor could I have confessed my blunder with such trust and equanimity. For the world that I had known was harsh and punitive and cruel, and consequently I had lived in it like a convict on the run. I think we all came out of it stronger and better in the end. For my part, having faced the pain of losing G, so long ago, with understanding from my group and the whole community, I felt the need to celebrate such warming generosity that I was receiving now both from within and from without. From this widening sense of freedom grew the urge to work on this book, with a heart that could at last confront darker ages that had passed.

But what of Cynthia, in her turn? She drifted round the Unit for some weeks in her dishevelled, tearful state, like an old lady adrift, in no condition to join any group for serious psychotherapy. Now this was not anything very new or unusual in our work. It frequently took weeks or months before some broken individual would renounce helpless confusion and exchange its hold and power for the task of settling down and getting well. But with Cynthia, it was all too clear that she felt that she had more to gain by staying a helpless child, the Unit's liability.

So Christmas slowly came in sight. Cynthia decided to go home, though all of us, the whole community of thirty patients and a sizeable staff tried to discourage her. We knew by then that Cynthia's family were not primarily concerned with her getting herself strong and well if such a course involved the dark disgrace of spending several years in a mental hospital; even in a special wing that was run in some respects more like a university. Neither had they seemed prepared, when I got in touch with them, to consider or support private psychoanalysis, though it was not a question of a lack of money in this case.

During her Christmas days at home, just as we had thought and feared, they simply told her to 'pull herself together now'. This inevitably led to new hatred on her part for being so little understood, and consequent readmission to the local mental hospital, just as we had predicted it. From there she wrote us pleading notes requesting that we negotiate her transfer to us in the south. This time she would really try to use the opportunity. But hardly was she back again than she packed her scanty bags and left. A man she had once known in Greece also had vested interests in getting Cynthia back again. He telephoned repeatedly, and wretched pawn that she was in all these people's complicated games, she flew off to Greece in a most precarious state. G, of course, was jubilant. For one thing she had proved me wrong in that self-defeating game of adolescent brinkmanship that nobody has ever won. Cynthia was going to be alright. The sea and sun and songs of Greece were the guarantee for that: phooey to psycho-therapy. G would spend her holidays speeding Cynthia back to health. She was going to see to that. Very often she would read me 'lovely letters' Cynthia had sent; incoherent little books rambling on and on and on about lovely sea shores, songs and love. There were these kennels she was working in, looking after Greek stray dogs. There was this love. There was this man, his lovely mother and some restaurant. Of her depression, not a word. It seemed that only I could see that these pages were not white, but black! So things continued for two more years until the news came: she was dead. Just off the mainland she had drowned.

Accounts varied naturally. Her family explained to G coldly, with much hostility, that there had been some accident. They spoke of currents and their treacherous strength. They blamed the coastguards, fishermen and Greece. They blamed the weather and the beach with a proud ferocity. Yanos, her lover, said instead that she had dived into the waves, in her usual spot, and had simply not come up again. She had been so happy, he believed. He could not understand it. Why? There was no reason, he maintained. Reading her letters once again, G found in them black despair. On this re-reading she did not discover any sun or song, only the endless will to die.

I know that the question will be raised whether I believe analysis could have mitigated these events. Could the stranglehold of death in her every cell have gradually been released to make way for its opposite – the affirmation of the gift of life? How can we hope to answer that when we have not been privy to that dark debate on suicide. Had Cynthia reckoned she would leave her cruel 'inner family' at the bottom of the sea and rise at daybreak, born again? Did drowning promise her a safe return to the undivided womb? Safe conduct to some preborn calm, the sleep no conflict can disturb? Had she believed that she would die? Had she invested all her life in this dark gesture of reproach and hate? Would she, in analysis, have mobilized her powers of love and independence in the end? Could she have found the patience, stood the pain to wrestle with her fury and despair, until she had won through, inch by inch, together with her analyst? Could she have shared the credit and reward with this new mother-father in her life? Or did she fear she might have grudged that breast its bounty as she had envied the first maternal breast, and in that manner found herself back at the starting post again? Was this, perhaps, her fantasy? There is no knowing. It is too late. An analyst can never be more than half a partnership, even if he needs to be the senior partner for a stretch of time.

But if it can be touch and go as in Cynthia's case, what are the preconditions for the other half to enter in? How was it that I was able, in my fraught distracted state, to somehow find my wavering way to my Jungian mother? How or why did I succeed when, at the start, I was as ill as Cynthia? The hieroglyphic answer is often inaccessible at an initial interview. Of course there can be evidence of the true investments that a given life has made on the side of hope and love. But finally so much depends on how those deeper battlefields and dispositions are aligned. How far communication lines reach back to something that was truly good, even though it may have lain dormant through the darkest years. We have our signposts, certainly. But they are mainly signposts in the dark. And therefore all we can do, as always when we are in doubt, every time the shadows fall, is to side resolutely with life. To dig our toes in on that shore for everything we are worth, from hour to hour and day to day, conscripting as a bonus all the willing hands and hearts and gifts that come along for the long climb. For there is nothing further that needs to be done to celebrate our presence on this earth. All of us are hourly recipients of benefits. We may or may not notice this. For me they laid a tiny path to my Jungian mother's house and on beyond it to a living day, the day that Cynthia never saw. I cannot explain the reason. But I can say with Eddington, the physicist, 'Something unknown is doing we don't know what.'

In the Beginning

All experience awaits recapture in the day to day of dreams, analysis and life. I remember being born. There was a splintering in the head, together with a bursting pain, a gurgling where there should have been breath, a feat of rescue and reprieve equally mysterious as that onslaught just before. This baffling sequence of events I have repeated all through life. Time and again, when all seemed lost, I somehow won through in the nick of time. When it was over there remained a blind necessity to sleep. To relegate this vast ordeal back to oblivion whence it made an illicit, brief escape. For everything has been inscribed in the computers of the mind from the beginning to the end.

'You almost died when you were born. You had that string twice round your neck and looked quite blue. Well, almost black. Ugly, really terrible,' my mother in due course confirmed this cataclysmic episode, during my analysis, one Sunday in her tidy flat.

Listening to her carefully I was unable to detect, fifty-three years afterwards, a trace of feeling in her voice, nor any hint that she had perhaps felt terror when her first-born did not cry in that impressive bedchamber of that villa in Berlin in which she too had grown up.

Since she had been accustomed to having all that money buys, which at the hour of my birth meant an obstetric galaxy, perhaps the possibility that something could go drastically wrong had not found its way into her mind. Or, if it had just flitted in, was simply bundled out again before the feeling had a chance to register its overtones. For Mother, now aged seventy-nine, got rid of fortunes in this way, habitually all her life, until very recently.

Until very recently, when my Kleinian analysis began to send a gentle rain, the deserts of this debris of feeling that she feared to own stretched between us, far and wide. Every time we were to meet I felt I was obliged to mount a full-scale expedition to traverse this blighted land. Yet, each time I set out again to visit, often fearing for my life, I slowly came to recognize that my growing sanity mobilized this enterprise and equipped it patiently to ensure I would survive several hours in this land which as I had once believed held no oasis anywhere. The only thing that I was no longer allowed to take, at that point, was an antidote to pain. I could no longer cast it out by being 'naughty', 'wild' or 'bad', all those awkward, stubborn things I had resorted to in the past, spilling, spoiling, injuring my belongings and myself with dreadful regularity.

'Who is the mother? Who the child?' my terror squealed continuously. 'Look, you grown-ups everywhere, my mother simply cannot cope.' This was the mother whom I loved so much, whom I worshipped and adored, and strove and struggled from the first to protect and to support, at the same time as I raged against her incapacity, until nothing but the rage remained. The love went hiding underground to be swept back in a dream.

I remember the rustle and papery starch of Nanny up against my cheek. And a swimming circle over me. Was it face or was it breast? Or the bottle in my Nanny's hand when after several horrid days, Mother abandoned the struggle and put my life in Nanny's charge. Was that the hovering shape above, to which I owe until this day a worship of great birds of prey that spread and circle overhead? Is it this that could explain Leonardo's memory of the tail of a great bird beating him across the lips early in his infancy: the straight, hard nipple and the breast gently swinging overhead, which must be the baby's view? What is the use of adult words? Before the tender age of three, I lost the Nanny of my life. All fell apart. Joy veered away, like the split atom navigates, shrieking down the lanes of death. For more than half a century I could bear nothing that was blue. And then, in my analysis, at last it swam before my eyes: her uniform had been blue. I had spent an aching life looking for my only love and the disappointment of every single glimpse of blue had made me hate the colour more.

But even before that disaster of my nanny's disappearance struck, a previous catastrophe had all but cracked my world apart. I was taken by the hand and led down those daunting corridors which kept the wings of our great house so heartbreakingly far apart. At my parents' bedroom door, flowering vistas greeted me. Extravaganzas of this kind meant that Father was at home. I saw my beautiful Mama like an angel, all in white, floating upon clouds of lace, among roses everywhere. I wanted, no, I insisted that I be picked up instantly and placed beside her on the bed, but was restrained and shown instead, by someone in the entourage, something that had now become the centre of the universe whose highlight I had been until then: a pink, a horrible pink worm. They say I cried out: 'tiny eyes', and did my best to poke them both out of the atrocious head of this pretender to the throne. But the deep reality was more sinister than that; a cataclysm which escaped detection for over fifty years.

It burst out of its well-built hiding place, by the purest accident, on a morning that I met a younger woman from abroad, also in treatment with my analyst, a 'couch-sister', as we say. We acted like two long-lost friends and soon dashed out to celebrate at a Brazilian restaurant because she wanted me to taste her traditional, native fare. From now on nothing in our lives would, I felt, remain unshared. But after lunch I grew depressed. My senses seemed to disappear. Thick layers of cotton wool were stuffed between me and the outer world. As the weekend dragged along I fought for reason, for my life. And yet there was no symptom that the Doctor-me could isolate: no temperature, no pain, no rash.

Then at last Monday crawled along. The analytic weekend plays a whole variety of tricks and Monday's session as a rule restores a balanced frame of mind. But matters went from bad to worse. Now I could neither see nor hear as I was lying on the couch. As rats will leave a sinking ship my senses were deserting me. Here was the end of all my dreams. What use was this analysis? My hopes that it would lead me out of confusion, step by step, died down around me, once again. In the old and dreary way I resorted to retreat: 'I am too serious a case. I am too old. I should have come, twenty, thirty years ago instead of wasting fifty years.'

Here was that bottomless, black hole which had dogged me all through life. I fled from the analysis during that Monday session in the blind, helter-skelter way that was my habit and my style. I felt I could no longer fight to save what I had once possessed in terms of mental clarity. As when a house is burning down, it was a case of salvaging – as it seemed to me that day – whatever swayed within my reach, except there was no longer an 'I', nor any 'he', or analyst. Only the gutted, charred remains of a former edifice, only rubble where there had grown the walls of a relationship. Where was a lifeline to that past? Words floated through the empty air. Yet when I tried to snatch at them, I could no longer link them up to make connections, rhyme or sense. Sense was dismantled, severed, stripped: the familiar categories deprived of every handle, grip or trust.

It took a week of patient analytic work to restore meaning, hope and love to these bombshell-like events. Meeting my younger 'sister' had triggered explosions in my mind of a previous baby's birth, since the unconscious does not have any cognizance of time. Here was the pink worm back again. And with it all the rampant fears of absolute maternal loss had hurtled me a second time straight through the 'autistic gate'. I was living for the second time through an autistic episode. It felt like having to undergo major surgery with no anaesthetist to hand.

As the analytic task grappled with the catastrophe during ensuing days and weeks, I realized that my analyst had suspected for some time that there must have been an autistic episode very early in my life. There had been dreams suggesting that the loss of the breast had hit so hard, once this brother hogged it all, that, inconsolable, I had replaced its warmth and comfort with anything and everything that could be stuffed into my mouth and sucked despairingly instead.

Now I had lived a second time through the fright of this eclipse that my brother's birth had meant. But if that lightning had struck when I was twenty-five months old, how was it that I had escaped the fate of total mind arrest? Who had resuscitated me? To whom did I, in retrospect, owe this debt of gratitude?

'Let us see,' my mother said, when I questioned her again.

It was a Sunday, as before, and it was raining quietly. Not an afternoon for strolling round the tidy park that adjoins her block of flats. I had been careful to avoid the actual word 'autism'. Had I been 'poorly', or 'distressed', soon after my brother's birth?

'Well, we shall look and see,' my mother said.

She seemed a little interested and wanted above all things else to be helpful to her child. This has always been the case. How she struggled all her life with her cruel ineptitude, who grew up

21

motherless herself from a very tender age! She got up from her leather chair with the slight difficulty that she has experienced ever since her hip replacement operation. I watched her as she slowly rose to her full majestic height and took some careful steps across to her fine six-foot-tall bookcase. There stand, carefully preserved, those remnants of her library which are most meaningful to her.

As she unlocked and opened it, I drew in the scent again, familiar from my childhood days, inseparable from old books when they are beautifully bound and have been lovingly preserved. Then they exhale in gratitude that musky, aromatic scent, and I inhaled it gratefully and felt extremely privileged. For it is not often that this polished glass case is unlocked when I am actually there – it is a sign of the growing trust there is between us nowadays. From the shelves my mother took a volume of the diaries that she had kept up day by day until, in 1938, she became a refugee. When the hour struck to flee, it was her diaries she had saved, when there was barely enough time to pack a nightdress and be gone.

She settled back into her chair and turned the pages that are bound in fine, red leather until she came to the first months of my life. There my weight from day to day stood registered and how much milk I had consumed, as Nanny had reported it.

'You see, what interest I took?' My mother's voice is strong and proud as we confront this evidence of well-discharged maternity. 'Aha,' now warming to her theme, 'a trip to Paris that we made. And here is Florence, where I went with your father, at the time. You were already six weeks old. Now, here we have your brother's birth, and here, yes, good, he cried at once. Now, you again, Yes, "tiny eyes", you said and tried to poke them out. You see, it's all recorded here.'

Because it is all recorded in such detail, conscientiously, we slowly gravitate towards the kind of information that I am looking for. 'Eleanore,' my name at that time, 'begins to run a temperature. The temperature goes on and on. Professor so-and-so is called.'

'He was a great authority on every matter of that kind,' my mother adds, consolingly, as if she needs to reassure a relentless enemy who never stops accusing her.

What is all this analysis? I very often feel her storm, antagonized and rather hurt. For does it not insinuate that she failed me in some way?

'Those men, you know,' she sometimes says, quoting her brother on the theme of analysts, 'know when they're onto something good. While the money lasts, of course.'

Mother and Uncle disapprove of people who are after other people's money. For they have found the world to be greedy and grasping, they maintain.

She turns the pages slowly now. 'Yes, we still have the temperature. And here, it says, you stayed in bed and only took a little soup: a spoon or two of consommé. Now here, the Herr Professor said that you might get up again, in the middle of the day. The temperature was coming down. He called it *Bewegungs Temperatur*.

I wondered what that word could mean, 'movement temperature'. Was that what today we would call psychosomatic or emotional? Meanwhile there seems nothing more that I would want to hear about: behaviour changes, mood and sleep. Nothing that gives a tell-tale hint of regression, at this point. Maybe Nanny noticed it but could not put it into words for the day-to-day report? Perhaps intuitively she felt that anxieties should be withheld so soon after my brother's birth, and meanwhile, very likely made all the right responsive moves to make those evil spirits pass before they took a lasting hold?

But since my mother had, it seemed, also found it difficult to recover from this second birth, the Professor suggested now that she should travel with my Nanny and me to the magical Engadine. Perhaps the Herr Professor was wiser than anybody knew. For it seemed that in St Moritz, the beneficial altitude and the healthy alpine sun made the mysterious fever yield.

Mother seems well satisfied. 'There, you see, it went away. We did the right thing, obviously.'

'Obviously you did,' I smile, in my mother's small, neat flat, where everything stays in its place, so unlike my London home.

Now I enjoy a deep relief. On behalf of that small girl I feel so grateful and at peace that in this crisis in her life, unable to protect herself except by overheating to produce the tell-tale temperature, she got her mother and her nurse absolutely to herself for several weeks on end, for the first time in her life, while that dreadful baby had been obliged to stay at home in the care of his own nurse.

Meanwhile Mother carries on, 'Your father joined us. You refused to recognize him at first. Only the next day. Well, how strange.'

To me, it is not strange at all. For now 'the enemy' was back, who wanted Mother to himself. Now he would take her far away and I would lose her once again. Yes, I would have to yield her up without a word in my defence.

'Your father took me to Copenhagen. And you went back then, to Berlin.'

She closes the red leather book. It is three-thirty, time for tea.

'You see,' she adds in her own defence, locking the glass book-case door, 'you always thought that I was not really, truly interested. Of course we travelled such a lot. People did in those days. Also, you must not forget, you had your Nanny, anyway.'

'I wonder when she left?' I asked.

'When you were ready for the next, I would imagine,' Mother smiled. 'Next time we will look at that. Would you like Indian or China tea? Have what you like, child. You can choose.'

Choosing is something quite, quite new, belonging to my fifth decade. Consequently I am still a little heady and surprised every time I exercise this startling possibility. During those first years, in Berlin, it came full circle once a year. On the second day in April, Cook would come to the nursery to take luncheon orders from me: the best of all my birthday gifts. There she would stand, enormous, white, red-faced and slightly out of breath, pencil poised above her pad; and I would say with majesty: 'spaghetti with tomato sauce'. I never wavered on my theme. Spaghetti was a solid link with the healing Engadine, the small pension run with the clockwork regularity the world was subject to in those days. My choice began and ended there, remaining the prerogative of kings and queens the other three hundred and sixty-four days of the submissive year; a tantalizing chink of light on which the darkness closed again when the empty dish went back to regions whence it had come.

The nursery had a padded door. Children frequently make noise. The handle of that towering door was too high for me to reach. It had its own perplexing laws in which my longings had no say. I could only moon around and watch that handle for a sign of life from the outer, happier world. If I watched it, long enough, I knew that it was bound to move. At bedtime, when they were not away in the four corners of the earth, parents came in evening dress, to wish us both a nice goodnight, briefly at each bed in turn, before Nanny showed them out. How beautiful the parents looked; they did not wear a uniform and smelled of flowers I had never seen. The others all wore uniform. The chauffeur's was dark navy-blue, adorned with buttons made of gold. Successive nannies had one too, after that initial blue, with hooks and eyes and safety pins. Maids changed from pink, to mauve, to black through the hours of the day, as though in keeping with the sky. Caps of white perched on their heads, like frills on a crown of mutton roast. Cook was always swathed in white on the occasions when she rose from her kitchens way below.

Food, which made the handle move, had to come up in a lift. The lift was very, very far from the nursery, of course. Three or four times every day, trays came within sight and reach. They were carried by a maid. Upon them rested silver cupolas like those on a Byzantine church. The maid would leave the tray and glide to pull the heavy padded door shut behind her, carefully. I am not certain whether she spoke. Perhaps she said, *Guten Morgen* or *Guten Apetit* but I cannot be positive. I feared that people would be sacked for speaking unless spoken to. This term had swum into my consciousness when I eavesdropped on the maids, an activity which was my most important source of knowledge of the outer world. From it, I built an image of who was who and what was what, though it often proved bewildering. Being sacked meant being pushed into an enormous sack like the bad wolf possibly, then maybe drowned or eaten up. I took great trouble not to be the cause of such a dubious fate and consequently I would meet silence with silence to the best of my stunned ability. The food had to be eaten up. Its colours were greens-green, carrot-orange, prune-brown, and pudding-white. But memory here is very cold. And memory is shivery just like the start of a bad illness, when the fever has just dropped, briefly, before coming back.

Between that nursery and Berlin lay great flights of marble stairs, and all the rooms and anterooms and ballrooms of the floor below. The cunning scent of hot-house plants and cellophane-ensheathed cigars would animate long galleries where dark,

25

imposing pictures hung and children rarely set a foot. Sometimes blueish wreaths of smoke danced together in the air unattended by a human shape. At other times, I caught a glimpse of ladies or of gentlemen who spoke in whispers as they gazed upon the pictures on the wall. Was it forbidden to speak loud – even where pictures were concerned? It made me feel very afraid of paintings locked into a frame for very many years to come.

The front door, once it had been reached, was like a drawbridge: difficult to master and negotiate. A porter in grey uniform operated this device, as part of his mysterious life, in a narrow little lodge where he spent his days and nights dedicated to that task. Every time we returned from the Grünewald or the Zoo he had to jump to it again. That was once or twice a day, depending on the weather and the delicacies of our health. In memory the weather is grey. Only rarely, if Mama or Pappi took us out, the weather had the colours of sun, wind and blue sky. But memories can also lie. Across their pearl-grey, pudding-white, I see the grown-ups shake their heads. 'Nini, you are distorting everything again. Why do you never speak the truth?' What do they mean, then, by 'the truth'? Can it be something different from the hot and cold I feel, the thumping of my tick-tock heart, the queasy lurching in my soul? In the marrow of my bones and in the place where stomachs lie, I feel each time they scold me, that they are very very hurt, at their wits' end over my wicked and ungrateful ways. That this time I am written off since I may never, never change and so am almost bound to be a burden to them all my life, because I keep inventing tales that no one in the whole wide world is able to substantiate.

My mother's maiden name was Rathenau. A relative called Walter, by that name, had scaled the heights of history. A Jew, he had achieved the status of Foreign Minister in the Weimar Republic. But since he struggled, undeterred, with a fine, free-ranging intellect, to change the mean and rigid assumptions of a defeated Germany, he was eliminated. In other words, this upright man, who remained sublimely free, for all that rattling of chains, was assassinated by the perpetrators-to-be of the Third Reich on their dark cavalcade to power, just as my subtle, innermost truth was slowly murdered by the frowns and disapproval that it drew, to leave me totally without that inner compass we require to steer our life by its own star.

But his was not the only corpse. I came across them everywhere, toes and fingers poking out from hasty, half-uncovered graves. Sometimes, on returning home, from these walks that were prescribed, I told Mother I had seen someone being killed stone dead. They had, I said, with flaming cheeks, been run over by a car and buried, without more ado, underneath a paving stone. Mother shook her weary head. What *was* the matter with the child? Why would she not tell the truth and keep inventing all these things? How I felt the cold, white dead piled around me everywhere in that dark, historic house. My mother's mother killed herself when Mother was a little girl. 'The boys,' said Mother, only recently, the first time that she spoke of it, 'were always, always being ill. The worry of it brought her down.' But I eavesdropped here and there on a very different tale that I cannot substantiate. It whispered of a love affair, a scandal of enormous scale. But there was nobody to ask. They were all as impervious to such questions from a child, as marble is to strawberry jam. And since there was no one to ask, love and suicide soon grew as mixed up in my own mind as politics and getting shot were in my mother's all her life.

Hence politics were not discussed, even though the swastika was clearly closing in on us, tail up, like a scorpion. That must also be denied. Besides, this dangerous logic ran, we were not like 'other' Jews, who 'came from Poland and the East' and went in for 'dirty tricks'. *Ost-Juden* was the shameful word in circulation at the time, the term the rabble-rousing Sturmer used and Mother when she wanted to wash her hands of frightening things, take on protective colouring and escape from all the dead.

My mother's brother killed himself when she was in her early teens. How can I substantiate the grapevine of the whispering maids, that Paris brothels and VD made this motherless tall boy blow his brains out as the only way to save The Family from disgrace?

Had I invented these dark tales? I felt the dead lived in the house. I tried to find them everywhere. But it was all so difficult since the handle of the door was too high for me to reach.

Once, I managed to escape. Unobserved I made my way, terror-stricken and alone, to my parents' private wing at the far end of the house. In their bedroom stood a chest from which protruded an enormous key of intricately wrought brass. Breathlessly I raised the lid. Inside Father Christmas lay smiling through his long, white beard! I had spoilt my father's game and made him angry, once again. There was no knowing how he knew. No doubt the very walls had eyes. Sometimes, in the early dusk, I saw them riveted on me. Yet Father seemed my only hope. The one bridge to reality, although I did not know it then.

Of course, there was another man. My bachelor Uncle Rathenau. He was a proper publisher who, with that entire concern, occupied a string of rooms just opposite the nursery. We would pass those offices on our outings to the park and when we returned again. Their doors would sometimes stand ajar quite unlike all other doors. My uncle had a secretary who was sometimes heard to laugh. And no one stopped her, what was more; nor did she wear a uniform. Memory says that Fraülein Qui looked as pretty as a doll, and was allowed to, what was more. By that I mean she was allowed to show that she was not a doll but full of complicated tricks. In my secret heart I clapped and whispered to myself 'Hurrah'. The large and costly dolls I had could open and could close their eyes and whisper 'Maaaaama'. That was all.

They were really like myself because I was expensive too. Dresses, blouses, socks and shoes, white or patent-shiny black, velvet-collared little coats, gloves and bonnets, scarves and muffs, were all exquisite, beyond words. Other children stopped and stared at such perfection in the Zoo. It made me feel uncomfortable. I wanted to be like the rest, but could never quite make out what the rest were really like. There were those in fairy tales, sometimes good and sometimes bad. The bad ones met with dreadful ends. The good ones, everybody loved. I had no doubt that I was bad because I lacked all certainty that I was loved by anyone. If I was loved, if that was true, why did they always go away and leave me in the nursery buried by that awful door? What were other children like? How was I going to find out? Children only rarely came to that dark house in Berlin. Ivy clung to all its walls. Perhaps they were as overgrown in a spellbound, age-old dream as the Sleeping Beauty's castle?

I spent hours, I spent years, waiting for a living prince. A sallow, solemn little girl, I hovered, where the curtains fell from the ceiling high above to the polished floor below, twisting the expensive stuff with two nervous, well-scrubbed hands, nose pressed hard against the glass, to catch a glimpse of sound and life, a glimpse of Father coming home. When the great, black car pulled up there was nothing I could do, prisoner of those four walls. But, at least, he was at home. And provided I was good and gave no cause for fresh complaints with a nasty mess or noise, then at bedtime he might come and stay just long enough to fill the stagnant air with his cigar, and float my floundering heart again before it just gave up and sank.

I understood that Father 'worked'. In Berlin I never saw money in its naked form; I felt uncertain whether 'work' was something good or something bad. As with my views on everything, day in, day out, I struggled to read Mother's face to take my cue. Money seemed to make her frown in a disdainful, irritated way, that I could not fathom in the least. But a different message ran that it was also sacred stuff. These two opposites would skip alongside in so many themes that my researches in the end left me nowhere. That was that. I would give the struggle up, bury the matter as a dog will bury a half-eaten bone, to dig it up another day. Whichever theme my baffled mind might aspire to pursue, hopefully, some later time returning to it furtively, it bumped across this burial ground of nibbled and obscure ideas like wooden wheels on cobblestones, defeated by the exercise, only to lose another spoke.

The maids would speak of money, though quietly, among themselves. They used a word which was 'price'. 'What is a price,' I used to muse. Prizes, I knew more about. Those I got for being good and punishment when I was bad. Everything, it seemed, revolved round being the one or the other except that I was never sure what constituted either view. My Bible, which was Mother's face, offered no consistency. That I was totally confused, to a dangerous extent bordering upon lunacy, was something else I did not know; and if I sensed the grown-ups were in a similar boat, my mind quickly rid itself of such a terrifying thought. For whatever thoughts I kept would sooner or later be expressed and usually led to punishment simply for being there. It seemed that thoughts as terrible as that most likely led to being killed, like my famous relative. He had been shot for his ideas; so I had picked up here and there. I had no wish to share his fate. But there was also something else that frightened me a great deal more – that was being sent away or being made to disappear.

This frightening possibility soon acquired precedents. The carnival that filled my mind – roses, puddings, muffs and dolls, cars and ballrooms, perfume, gowns, the various graves and uniforms, different faces that poked out, all the strange mysterious rules, foibles, laws and etiquette, offices and padded doors – what was it all about after Nanny disappeared?

While Nanny existed there was a truth. That truth was Nanny. She was there. Blue and crackly white of starch, a face that flowed into a smile, benevolence that was dispensed regardless of this 'good' and 'bad', that did not measure worth in words but said, 'I'll have you, as you are; you see, I do not go away, even if you mess the bed, or your white dress, or socks, or shoes . . .' But later . . . when she disappeared?

The following day we got 'The Miss'.

Before my father lived with us, he had had another wife and lived in England. So I heard. He had liked England very much. More than he liked Germany although that was where he had been born, in Frankfurt to be precise. Where my father was concerned, there was a chance to be precise. Mysteries, of course, there were, but nothing really to compare with the ones surrounding those he had come to live among, who were called The Family. His parents lived in Hamburg then. Once or twice he took us both there to visit 'the old people', as Mother called them. He took his children on a train without a Nanny or a Miss. It was a risk he sometimes ran. On those occasions I would feel almost human. If he felt I did not always need a guard I could not be so very dangerous. Besides, it was a great relief to have two grandparents who could clearly be accounted for, just as father would account for England, which he liked so much.

Father loved all things English, like Dover sole and marmalade, and English nannies known as 'Miss', a view I found I could not share. On Sundays, if he was at home, we would savour 'Sunday Fish' in the special 'breakfast room'. It came on a long silver dish, provided Father did not have to be away on 'business trips'. These, whatever they might be, became more frequent at this time, which meant that Sunday Fish became something of a rarity.

30

Nanny first. Father next. Both were made to disappear in quick succession. One, two, three! And they no longer lived with us – that is to say The Family. Everything we had was theirs. All the carpets, all the rooms, all the pictures on the walls – of which people spoke in whispers – all the silver, the damask, the porcelain and the chandeliers, the marble and mahogany, the plants, the trappings and the cars ... Brother and sister known to me as Uncle and Mother, it was they, and they alone, who composed this entity. There was no way of finding out if it included me as well; possibly, when I was good. Had my father then been bad, if he was no longer there with the scent of his cigars? The Family had borrowed him for some mysterious purposes and then got rid of him again. So, at least, it seemed to me.

The situation and the pain did not have a nursery name. The Miss, the second or the third, sat wrapped in silence, like the rest. Perhaps she did not even know that we had had a father once. And Mother never mentioned him. It may not have occurred to her that a father, lost and gone, was a matter of concern to the children. 'The children of Frau Morgental' was what we had now become.

But deep within my heart I knew that I was Father's child as well and that my father was not dead. Even if they had no name, I knew the corpses off by heart. They had a substance in the eyes of Mother and of Uncle Ernst. I read them, like an open book, dark and sombre as they often were, although the sadness was denied. Why be sad if you were rich and had so many, many things? I knew my father was alive because he lived inside my heart, in which he had a solid place. My image of him may have been the troubled and mysterious one of a semi-absentee. But it had sound and feel and smell which was more than others had. No, my father was not dead.

Since there was no one to ask and nobody who seemed to share my longing or anxieties, like a little dog I sniffed at doors and corners for a sign: cigars, black suit, his hands, his smile ... After an eternity the chauffeur found where Father lived. A flat was something new to me. Why must other people live downstairs and upstairs in this house? But there was very little time to establish any truth about these latest mysteries. When lunch was over, all too soon, the Herr Chauffeur was back again. He had come to put us back behind the massive, padded door. But now, at any rate, I had Father's promise that we might come for Sunday lunch again, even if nothing had been said about when 'again' might be in the baffling scheme of things.

Father now lived in a flat. I wanted to live there as well. It seemed more cosy and there was no one in a uniform, no Miss or Nanny, maid or cook. It was a revelation when Father cooked the lunch himself, meat, potatoes, everything. I had never even seen a kitchen in my life before. Cook consistently refused to let me enter her domain. 'Kitchens,' she would sternly say, 'are not for little boys and girls.' So to live with Father now seemed a beautiful idea. If he did not live with us, then he could belong to me. I would have him for myself and learn to cook him lovely things. We would leave The Family, who did not want us anyway.

Dreams fated for a crash . . . Father had quite different plans. Father now had other girls, I realized when we went again. In some respects they seemed quite nice, though difficult to tell apart behind the rouge, the pearls, the black, the smiles, the perfume, the fur and kid; only that my white shoes and socks, even my favourite white dress, were absolutely not a match. That was all too evident. Now fury seized my childish heart. I cut it open there and then to rip my father out of it, for ever, if possible. As it turned out, I could not, which in the end was just as well or it might have shrivelled up through the years that lay ahead.

In this way Father kept his place, which he doubtless deserved, though soiled by my despair and hate, my fury and my jealousy. It was a dirty little nest in which the 'other' girls in black lay cut up into little strips, a gory Jack-the-Ripper scene spattering my inner world.

But as it happened, Hitler had no time for broody little girls. All at once the Reichstag burnt. Angertatta told me so.

She was my mother's childhood nurse. Her room adjoined our nursery and she was not supposed to fill our heads with 'rubbish of that sort'. Generally she kept the rule in obvious fear of banishment. But on that Sunday the flames and smoke had sent her scuttling back at once, unable to contain herself. 'Thank God, it was not the Dom', her beloved House of God, but a mere parliament of men whose ashes fluttered through the air.

Then, upon a cold, dark day – Mother must have been away – Father came and took us out in the middle of the week. What could have happened, ran my fears, just below the waves of joy? March was the month. The year was 1933. After midnight my eight-year-old domain would vanish like a puff of smoke. My white-gloved hand would never again lie in my father's silk-gloved one, in the back of that great car which smelt of leather and cigars. The car whose usual right of way was cut to a snail's pace on that day, as faces that were insolent and mean and itching fingers pressed against the shining bodywork and gleaming glass. It was as though a solid fence, no, a whole barricade had broken down, as if a long-postponed stampede had burst through the resulting gap to within inches of our lives. At midnight, wholly unexplained, the world that I had known was squeezed into a sleeper on a train that was bound for Switzerland and the familiar pension, while Father vanished once again into that hole that had no name.

Why had Berlin disappeared? It was quite obvious, from the start, that this was not a holiday. Along with everything else the latest Miss had stayed behind. There was Mother now, instead. But why the middle of the night? Why no time to pack some toys? Who was the lady wrapped in furs who was travelling with us? In certain ways she seemed like one of Father's recent girls in black, with powder, satin, rouge and pearls. 'One doesn't need that sort of thing,' Mother's comments used to run contemptuously in the past. But all at once she had a friend whose need for these absurdities was very clear and evident, and tolerated, what was more. She seemed like certain hot-house plants that need to be wrapped in cellophane. That did not worry me too much. But what was really bad and unendurable in the fact was that the two of them seemed wrapped up in each other in a way that left no room for anyone else. All very well to lose the Miss, but now came the catastrophe of having nobody at all. Only a mother who was quite visibly there, but who clearly had no time to spare.

That was more than I could bear, especially since Mother cried like a frightened child that night. I heard her, as I lay awake, through the rumbling of the train. I would have also liked to cry, but it was useless when there was no one in the whole, wide world who would have even noticed it or handed me a handkerchief. For it was obvious from the start that this treasured, silky friend was a write-off as far as children were concerned. Nor did this change through the six years during which she and Mother would become entirely inseparable. Each seemed the other's favourite child and mother rolled into one and there was nothing, nothing left for anybody left outside.

After several weeks had passed in the familiar pension, a German governess appeared. She had a nasty, scowling face and said she would look after us but hoped that we would behave. She liked nothing very much and children, clearly, least of all. For some nine months she walked us, every day, round the deep St Moritz Lake with a sullen, spiteful face. She felt that she was being paid to exercise the little brats. It seemed that she had no idea where our missing mother was or what had happened to the slinky friend.

During those nine, endless months, everything died inside my heart. Father was gone I knew not where, together with the girls in black. Mother had someone better too, and she too had disappeared. Nanny was never coming back, that seemed painfully clear. My little brother and myself seemed all alone in all the world. This Fräulein simply did not count. There was no single part of her that a child who suffered from a broken heart could utilize.

And yet the sun broke through once more. Or was that hard, white light the sun – with its baffling, crazy gleam?

'Children, we are going home.' Mother simply reappeared, straight out of the wintry snow. It was spring when we had come to the sheltering Engadine.

'To Berlin?'

'No, you will see. Somewhere much more beautiful.'

Her face was shining, new and bright. Home would be Bavaria now. Not far from Berchtesgaden as the blackest crow might care to fly.

At least we had a home once more. Ravenous for ownership, if it meant stability, I drank the novel beauty in, the pines, the meadows and the peaks that framed this picture-postcard farm. With its green shutters and low-pitched roof weighted down with heavy stones against fierce winds and heavy snows, a hollowed tree trunk at the door through which the icy waters ran from a hidden glacier source, it was small wonder that Mother had lost her heart to a fantasia she herself must have longed for as a child cooped up in that sombre house among the shadows of the dead. There it snuggled, on a slope of apple orchards reaching up to secret forests of blue pine, cool in summer and in wintertime a refuge from the blustery storm, offering shelter to the hare and deer whose tracks across new-fallen snow we slowly learnt to tell apart.

The farm was still a going concern in a local farmer's care. A woman who tended some thirty cows lived in a poky room next to the animals. But, best of all, poor Rosel had two children of about our age. At first I could only stare at them. Children in Berlin would come with their nannies all dressed up to take hot chocolate in the afternoon. Or they came for birthday parties when we all sat nice and still while a magician conjured things like doves and rabbits from a hat. We never played and never spoke, as far as I could remember now. I think the nannies spoke for us, hovering with a comb or sponge to keep us respectable through the proceedings to please the twittering mamas who were taking tea below in the little tea salon where important people met.

But here were children with their hair unkempt, barefoot and in makeshift clothes. We stared at them and they stared back, a situation that was fraught with danger and with ecstasy for all parties probably.

Hansi broke the silence first.

'Can you spit as far as me, to that grey stone over there?' he asked my brother testily.

Ello only shook his head and took a few steps back in fear.

'We are not allowed to spit,' he managed painfully, at last. 'I'd better go into the house.'

I, on the other hand, was brave. I had waited all my life for such an opportunity.

'I can spit quite far,' I lied.

'Let me see, then,' Hansi crowed, in Bavarian dialect.

I cast my eyes towards the house with all the passion of a prayer. Nobody was watching me, then spat I for all that I was worth.

'That's good,' said Hanni. 'You're quite good.'

She stared at me approvingly, amazed that somebody in shoes and socks and with ribbons in her hair came up to scratch in this respect.

Freedom hovered in the wings, insubstantial as a moth. But freedom was to be curtailed. For reasons nobody explained it seemed that we could not attend the local village school, so a teacher was in residence from the hour we arrived; Mother had seen to everything. She was a lady who had lost her job, at a secondary school, for 'something that she could not help'. Now she faced the prospect of opening two scuppered minds to the soothing beauty of supreme coherence in all things. It could have been no easy task to usher this new era in, but Mother seemingly approved.

To underpin coherence we would be Bavarian children now, in Bavarian national dress, the 'dirndl' and the leather pants. I learnt the zither. Once a week a music teacher came along on a sturdy bicycle with a feather in his hat. It was, I thought, extremely nice, being a Bavarian child. It meant you learnt to ski and skate, to climb tall mountains and to swim. There wasn't so much sitting still, nor had I ever been averse to getting a pretty dress. Being a Bavarian child also meant you were confirmed. Hanni got these snow-white things and white flowers in her hair and carried candles to the Church in procession – beautiful. Why could I not have the same? When there was nobody around she let me slip this magic on just to see how it would feel. If I was a Bavarian child, why was my white dress withheld? If I was a Bavarian child, why must I be different in unforeseen, bewildering ways, that fell like hail from summer skies?

One innocent Bavarian day, a strange, unlikely-looking man climbed out of Mother's big, blue car that drew up in a cloud of dust. Black coat, black beard, black eyes, a black hat which he would not hear of taking off, even when inside the house, the ambience of this latest guest was of a mourner from some different land. No such apparition had materialized before my eyes even in the most furtive fantasies.

'Take the Rabbi to your room upstairs and please be sensible and good. Nini, you are the older one. You know how ill your brother was, only very recently. We owe everything to God.'

Mother hastily withdrew and I knew better than to ask for a meaning anyway.

Seated upstairs at the desk I tried to keep my tears in check. The stranger seemed to break my heart by touching slack, forgotten strings no one had warned me that it had. What was it that he conjured up which I had a right to but had lost? Was it a father? Was it roots? The answer to some mystery? But like the mountains, mysteries stood around me on all sides.

'It is,' said he, 'your mother's wish that I instruct you once a week in Hebrew and the Old Testament, because, of course, as you both know, these are things a Jewish child needs to be familiar with.'

Whatever was a 'Jewish child'? But I was too afraid to ask a 'stupid' question and 'waste time'. We started with the alphabet. The Rabbi wore a kind, sad face, as white as a Sunday tablecloth. Etched across it, sharp, resigned, with indelible dark ink, showed a deep, despairing pain, that also, as I dimly sensed and for reasons that eluded me, concerned my brother and myself. Perhaps, I hoped, the answer lay in this daunting Hebrew tongue if only I could master it. Oh, what was wrong with him, I sighed. What was this sorrow in his heart like the big stones on our roof? Why did he sometimes gaze at us, as though he was about to cry? I realized that he stank with fear, regardless of the fact that stink was a quite forbidden word except for farmyard animals. Mysteries were as familiar as daisies by then, but this very latest one opposed me darkly, like a poisonous plant which thrives on dangerous, sinking soil to claim the unsuspecting life.

Mother was not always there to fetch him from the Munich train; on those days Ello and I had to do it, but on foot. We were wholly unprepared for what this latest order meant. Hanni and Hansi fairly stared. Other people stared as well and tried to look the other way. Some said '*Jude*' angrily and spat with venom as we passed, though I knew that spitting was very rude; it had been drummed into my head. My world of manners was transformed from one instant to the next, as on that morning in Berlin when Father took us when he went to vote. Had the Rabbi brought this on? Was he a '*Jude*'? What was that? Were we then, '*Jude*', as he claimed? Was our God different from Hanni's then? In any case, what was a God? But there was no one I could ask, for Mother would be furious if she got to hear of it, as was invariably the case. And if I made her furious, as I did quite frequently, by doing very dangerous things such as playing with the scythe and nearly cutting off a foot, or sledging downhill much too fast so I had to shout 'look out' to workers trudging home from work, I would be ordered to undress, which meant that she would use the birch. This crushed my spirit even more than it bruised my seat, humiliating each square inch of my rebellious entity. Consequently I would keep all my questions to myself. Even the most burning kind were, out of expediency, simply stuck onto the pile of festering bewilderment with little prospect of relief.

After something like a year, the gentle Rabbi disappeared just as Nanny and my father had done. Never would his soft, black beard stroke against my tingling cheek as he bent over to correct my work, his long, white finger pointing at the Hebrew page from right to left. I knew for certain he was dead, because the feeling had returned, in the midst of Bavaria, of corpses that nobody names, of people knocked down in the street and buried under paving stones everywhere you look and turn, even if invisible to those who claim that they know best.

My enthusiasm waned for being a Bavarian child. I would have liked it well enough if those people had not spat and had let the Rabbi stay alive to keep on coming to the house. I somehow sensed he held a clue to something I would have to know. It seemed a case of life and death. But once again, life did not pause for a single, wholesome breath because in 1936 the two of us were sent away.

Children stood on Mother's list of responsibilities. Dispositions must be made and then reviewed at intervals. Lawyers and accountants dealt with the inanimate estate; she made arrangements for the rest. For the second time within three years we found ourselves on a mysterious train. England was the destination, we discovered halfway there, the country that my father loved. Would he be waiting for us there? But to ask was not allowed.

On the boat and on the train Mother sat with that straight back and set expression on her face that boded rather less than good. I read the signs as '*occupé*', a sign the toilets on the trip showed each time the door was locked, from inside presumably; this suspicion was confirmed if I waited long enough for new developments. It was the only way of finding out what was what and how and why.

On the Channel I was sick. 'The child is sea-sick,' people said and handed me a paper bag. I did not look at Mother's face. At the other English end, I caught no glimpse of Father's shape in the various, swaying crowds, each of which I scrutinized every time the onward rush gave an opportunity to claim and hold a quiet spot until one hurried on again amidst semi-foreign tongues, porters, drivers, taxis, trains, ladies, children, gentlemen, passports, tickets, smoke and rain, sooty fingers, sky and grass. When the grass at last remained, Mother said, 'This is your School. I am going home again.' Within two minutes she had gone with a glazed and tearful face.

The school was a paradise. Its name was Bedales. Mother wished to have us both beneath one roof. Henceforth, three times every year, the children of Frau Morgental would make this same trip, to and fro; three times a year by aeroplane, 'Because,' as Mother said, 'they may fall out of ships and railway trains.'

This sky-lift sent me into complete delirium for two years. *Verboten* is a German word that knows of no equivalent in any other human tongue. It had been lifted suddenly. The Channel was the great divide. Here, on the new side, broke a dawn of sparkling possibilities. Back there, my puny, struggling self was time and time again wiped out if it so much as raised a finger. The miracle was that it still kept making the attempt, at intervals, although in terror for its life and only when nobody saw.

But as the starving dream of food only to find they cannot eat when the ordeal comes to an end, despite this heaven-sent relief, I missed my mother cruelly. By virtue of her ordering each detail of my waking life – the clothes I wore, the words I said, the silences I had to keep at mealtimes and especially when her friend desired rest, I had assumed that we were one and therefore indivisible. If we were separated now, this must imply a punishment, the one of being sent away that I had dreaded all my life, even while expecting it with a fatal certainty. If I seized life now with both hands, these new-found possibilities, would she still have me back again? I rather feared that she would not. And yet some small part of myself, that tried to speak up for the rest, cried, 'Take this opportunity. Enjoy these possibilities. Come on now, seize the living day.'

I took both courses: rushed ahead and simultaneously held back, appeasing either point of view. With a blind and furtive greed, a part of me latched onto this new bounty, labelled 'Yes, you may', while another sided with '*Es ist verboten*' as before. The left hand had simply no idea what the right was trying to do. I began to paint and write with feverish intensity, saying, 'Look, what I can do, if you tell me it's alright.'

How surprised I was to find willing allies in the staff. Adults on my side who said, 'Jolly good there'. And 'Well done' instead of 'Wrong' or 'Please be quiet'. Here was a sun that shone by night. Perpetual delirium. Boundless possibilities. In the obsolescence of what would one day be myself, I recognized with ecstasy that someone seemed to be at home. And yet, another part held back. What was the use of going free if some other half of me, called Mother, had remained behind, a victim of the endless fears no one spoke about. For the bravado which Mother wore was like an artificial limb.

When our Bavarian washerwoman sometimes drew me to one side and stroked my hair with her rough hand and sighed, 'Poor Nini, you poor child', I almost knew just what she meant. But then I did not want to know. What is the good of knowing things it is not possible to change? What is the use of dreaming of change when it stands written in the sky that one shall never, ever have the slightest say in anything – less than a puppy or a butterfly? And since I had no say in things and had to submit to every fate, the two years that bubbled like a heavenly brook ran towards an early end, as all good things had always done in my battered book of life.

Windows through which the sun had streamed were closed and shuttered once again. The Bedales dream came to an end. In July of 1938 Mother found she had no choice but to trade her name and fortune in for survival, neither more nor less. Her passport had not been renewed when she applied for it. And unsigned letters had arrived threatening to burn down her dream of a Bavarian sanctuary. A dream, which to that very hour no one had dared rattle at, so absolute was her belief that she was entitled to remain the one exception to the Führer's rule.

We had become three refugees on Europe's trembling and dismantled soil. Our circumstances had remained exceptionally adequate, compared with ladies who had become domestic servants overnight. We had an income that a working man might well have reckoned close to wealth, but Mother felt that having less meant having nothing left at all, since she knew only white or black and could not contemplate that grey has an infinity of shades. She could muster no affection for the faceless little house in an anonymous, suburban street where the city reached the fields. And when the outbreak of the war surprised the friend whom she adored visiting her native soil – since she was an Aryan – this was the final blow. She had lost fortune, country, name, importance, power and prestige, but these seemed as nothing when set beside the loss of this partner, whom she had endowed with the maternal radiance of an altar-piece, a loss which was to last for the duration of a bitter war whose final outcome stood in fearful doubt. Friendless, homeless, servantless, she had, with only modest means, to survive a total war on her every front: a helpless child thrown to the wolves with only pebbles to defend herself and two children in her care. That this predicament was bliss compared to the alternative of a concentration camp, I do not think she ever grasped, since she equated punishment with a crime that brought it on. Faceless evil she denied with absolute self-righteousness despite the massive evidence supplied by human history.

Against this background tinged with nameless dread and fraught with the realities of war, I began my teens. Like my Nanny in the past, so Bedales simply disappeared. And just like Nanny's patch of blue, the golden aura it had left tarnished slowly through the heavy years. The girls' school, with its high, brick walls, its concrete playground skirted around with iron railings, painted black, froze me like a prison camp, after the open Bedales fields. The inmates wore a uniform, including tie and blue felt hat, which defeated all attempts at appearing feminine.

My breasts were showing by this time. I had begun to menstruate. Ever since her mother's death, Mother had equated love and love affairs with suicide. The all-female, spinster staff seemed to share that view. Life was geared to passing exams, to academic excellence, and not a single man in sight.

Father wrote, from time to time, from an address that said 'New York'. Between us U-boats prowled the seas. But deeper than the submarines, lay unspoken the command not to speak my father's name. That implied disloyalty, barbarous ingratitude for a mother's total love amounting to self-sacrifice. I knew better than to protest that I had been stigmatized. In our bleak and lonely house there were no words for all the hurt that made you lie awake at night with an empty, aching heart, wishing that tomorrow would just go away and never dawn with its black and shabby face, its cold and hungry and despairing stare from a fixed and spiteful eye. And so the lease of war dragged on with the paralysing fear of a German victory.

The advent of internment camps blurred the finer difference between a Nazi and a Jew. English neighbours, on all sides, shunned this blighted family of 'Germans' living in their midst. They stayed behind their garden hedges, each on his own square of lawn. A voice, the walking of a dog, past our windows in the dusk, seemed the only signs of life on the other, native side. While most other refugees huddled into kinship groups, we were Jews who were no Jews, Germans whom the Germans did not want, and no more English, at the time, than the elusive Edelweiss with its lonely habitat on the inhospitable rock far from more convivial plants.

True, a very small elite of Jewish intellectuals had made for our city at the same time. These were vigorous families whose skills in science or the arts eased them into local life with every enviable show of belonging once again. But Mother, who in her own eyes had lost all position since she linked this fancy butterfly with wealth, would more willingly have died than make a tentative approach to ease our dismal loneliness. Sometimes daughters of this group signalled to me with a nod or smile that they wanted to be friends. But I preserved my frozen stance, afraid that they would pity me if I gave them half a chance to draw closer and inspect this outpost of catastrophe.

The unattractive little house, spotty-faced with pebbledash, was spartan to the last degree. Servants gone, the duster must not encounter obstacles on its daily duty round in Mother's unaccustomed hands. In consequence my bedroom struck so cold and clinical a note, which I felt as such a fall from grace, that I could not bring myself to let anyone at school gaze upon this festering wound, and – my greatest fear of all – take advantage of my abject wretchedness upon this score.

Nor was this the only one. Food was rationed for us all. But we no longer had a cook. What was it, then, that Cook had done to turn potatoes black with earth, carrots with whiskers, warts and tops, meat as red and raw as blood into warm, enticing meals? She was not there to answer that. And while my hunger made me eat the undercooked or charred results of Mother's first, enforced experiments, a relentless sense of shame lest all this should become known and spread about the school to be used as a taunt, compounded my unwillingness to strike any friendship up with those other, lucky girls, whose mothers doubtless baked and did what – in my cold, despairing eye – mothers the whole world over should.

Besides, I had no time for friends, as my mother needed help to man this semi-sinking ship. I sensed it with despairing love, an overwhelming sense of shame on her and on my own account, tinged with self-pity and scorn. Had she been able, only once, to share her terror through those years, to entrust me with those cares, which I could read in any case, what a relief it might have been. If only once we had wept, mother and daughter entwined, as countless others at the time, in their frustrated womanhood, what healing might have taken place. But neither could strike the spark for lighting this single beacon on such a blighted scene. Each kept a cold, stiff upper lip. And while my brother went to boarding school, two beings of a single sex, separated by no more than the merest twenty years in age, froze and hungered for one sip of love under exile's shabby roof.

Most certainly I had time off, like other girls, to go to school, or to the games field, or to swim; but over each domestic absence hung my pestering anxieties about this mother-child left all alone with nobody to comfort her. They ruled each minute that I snatched, as from some woeful contract I had never signed, yet felt enslaved by totally.

But while one part of me was thus subdued, some slumbering other half rose up with murderous life-force and rebellious wrath. So furious was its hellbent and blind desire for revenge, not knowing there was none to blame, that it laid waste the best intentions for countless years to come, as I played truant in my heart from true responsibilities, overburdened as I was by these imaginary ones.

It will come as no surprise that my school performance left everything to be desired. The headmistress and Mother shared the hope I might bestir myself, as 'School Certificate' approached, to get the minimal results required to become a nurse. To this dual conspiracy I remained an absentee in spirit and in attitude. I seemed unable to accept that these solemn, urgent plans could possibly concern myself since I was wholly unprepared to face the task of growing up and therefore of contemplating a career. But then, one fine day, I woke up and not a single hour too soon. 'Who wants to be a nurse?' thought I, deep in my rebellious heart. 'I might as well become a nun.' The prospect struck me as a bleak exchange of one dark prison for another; of uniform for uniform, brown stockings in exchange for black; horror for horror, lack for lack, hunger for hunger, end for end. I simply had to save myself and there remained one solitary path out of the approaching trap.

The school I hated was still 'good' by the academic standards of the day. Given a certain turn of mind, knowledge can be acquired by rote. And since examiners, then as now, tend to be impressed by a display of this ability, dangerous as it can be in total isolation from tempering human attributes, it carried me headlong into a place at London University which was then evacuated to the sheltering provinces. For the second time, in my elusive life, fate had somehow intervened. Its jerking arm had hijacked me, topsy-turvy and confused, to Leicester where, ostensibly, I was to read for a BSc.

But my deeper self, it seemed, had its own priorities. With its longer memory of freedoms won and snatched away, it soon drew up a different scheme, according to which I must at once find someone to take care of me for the remainder of my life; someone strong enough to wrench the leading reins from Mother's hands before two months of summer vac closed the prison gates to leave me at her mercy once again – how I construed her fraught attempts to have me qualify for a career while at the same time standing guard over my virginity.

This dual enterprise she saw as the quintessence of the task that she must honourably discharge: to get this daughter off her weary hands and launch her with decorum on the tricky seas of an alarming life, without such dowry as would guarantee the blessings of a gilt-edged match. These were the manoeuvres that I was determined to subvert, for I read them as a conspiracy to cramp my own, determined style.

And so, one hundred miles from home, my inner schemer lost no time in sizing rescue-workers up to meet my heady ends. No one seemed to fit the bill. Inexperienced and raw, sensible and serious, an elopement hardly seemed a top priority for fellow students in my year. At long last, as the spring approached, searching through the final year, a likely candidate appeared. A refugee, just like myself, he had obtained his BSc and was engaged on some

44

research. Penniless and all alone – his parents had not got away – with his dashing continental suits he somehow managed to project a masterful self-confidence that simply took my breath away.

It was springtime when we met. The sun shone on the hemisphere. Opulent lilac swayed in bloom. The pearly evenings were suffused with perfumes from the Arabian Nights. The summer vac was drawing nigh. He looked so handsome, brave and strong, yet at the same time needed me with a familiar urgency. As unspoken as my mother's kind, it promised me a well-known role and the ambiguous guarantee of indispensability. Even if I had nothing else in all the world to offer him for kindly taking me away, I could convey with all the skill of my wretched expertise that I could manage anything and everything that was required to make substantial stuff of dreams. Like Rumpelstiltskin I could spin the straw of dire reality into the gold that he required to follow his ambitious paths to be a doctor, when he lacked every shred and particle of means: an alien in an alien land waging an all-consuming war on each and every island front. And when my fine prince gazed at me through overpowering spectacles, and said, 'How you are beautiful,' I knew, beyond all realm of doubt, that he would love me to my dying day provided that I got to work with my little spinning wheel, which I was overjoyed to do.

It soon transpired that that this bargain had in decency to have the seal of sexual intercourse. My prince assured me brazenly that he was wonderfully *au fait* with all the ins and outs – even precautions against pregnancy – and that I need not be afraid. If the worst came to the worst, he knew a Jewish doctor who could terminate a pregnancy. In fact, he sometimes helped him out during holidays; a doctor could not start too soon on the vocation of his life.

For several weeks I hesitated. 'My mother says that it is wrong,' I offered lamely once or twice, dangerously near the brink. And 'Should we not be married first?'

'Mothers never understand,' he countered grandly, blow for blow.

'That's true,' I said it from the heart.

But terror lamed my every limb. Was it not because of sex that my mother's brother had killed himself? Was he not eighteen at the time, just my present age. And was it not because of love that my mother's mother took her life? The scales dipped gravely on the side of fear and deeply buried fantasy. But heavier, on the other side, lay the great emergency: the helter-skelter need for flight, together with the seething wish to show my mother, once and for all, who was the master in my house.

If I had never had a say in matters that concerned me most, then I would seize that say by force. If she had scared me, all my life, with veiled, atrocious prophecies connected with the marriage bed, then I would prove the old witch wrong. Besides, I feared that my poor prince would soon come to some dreadful harm if I continued to deny what he must have so urgently, or that he would be driven into someone else's arms, or a brothel possibly, and leave me, lonely, in the lurch.

The minute that I had scraped through the first part of my BSc I took the black bull by both horns. I yielded my virginity and took the very next train home to boast of this bravado to my poor mother there and then. It is a wonder I did not bring with me the two blood-stained sheets that the Bavarian peasants hung from farmhouse windows for the world to see the consummated sacrament. There is a straw for every camel's back.

The war was entering its fifth year that sultry summer, 1943. My mother's grip on sanity was slowly slipping, although neither she, nor I, nor anyone on this helter-skelter earth recognized the deepening cracks. And at this moment in her life, when she most needed some respite, she was instead confronted with the ultimate catastrophe which she had dreaded since my birth. She did not have a single friend with whom to share her deepest fears. Those acquaintances whom she had made from among spinsters, twice her age, who lived in local crevices, as harmless and leathery as lizards and at least as shy, would doubtless have been frightened off for ever by such blighted news. Their main concern was for their cats, all of them saved by surgery from the vagaries of sex. Not one of these high-minded souls would ever have come for tea again, with clockwork regularity, to brighten Mother's dreary years, had this scandalous event reached their hearing aids.

'Then marry him, at least,' she cried on the verge of a collapse.

But my prince had other plans when confronted with this prayer.

'I do not marry anyone I am not able to support.'

Mother's dark, perennial fears promptly bristled at this hint she had expected all along. While I, in my befuddled state, applauded these high sentiments.

'In that case, kindly leave my house,' said my poor mother to her erring child.

I packed such scraps as I possessed in a little leather case. I also took my bicycle. In my Post Office savings account slumbered ten or fifteen pounds that I was not supposed to touch – but who was going to stop me now? My prince possessed some pound notes and several shillings and half-crowns, more than enough to storm the world together with my spinning wheel whose true name was omnipotence. And so I left my mother's house, half jubilant and unafraid because my mind could not support the weight of its anxieties.

We walked the four miles into town and climbed aboard the London train that was bursting at the seams with khaki 'tommies' for the Front. They shared their beer and fags and crisps and undistilled euphoria, and sang as though to drown the burst of rifle fire and of shells already hammering in their ears: 'I'm going to hang out the washing on the Siegfried Line . . . if the Siegfried Line's still there.' Boom. Boom.

When this carnival on wheels pulled into Paddington at last, London loomed to welcome us. Through those years of trials of strength she rose superb before all eyes. Blitzed and buried, burned and bombed, smoked and molested both by day and night, she had become a fount from which her subjects drew draughts of courage for the coming day. If London stood, then so could they. And if they could, then why not we with each new morning as it came?

Evacuation had ensured a plentiful supply of flats at negligible rents and not too many questions asked. The Food Office supplied us with the necessary ration cards and also with our monthly 'points' for foods that were in short supply. For something like four pounds a week it seemed quite possible to live and live we both would, come what may! Such was the gratitude I felt for 'being taken care of now', that I took care of everything. I quickly found myself a job as a sales-girl in an East End shop. I cycled there and cycled back all the way from Bayswater and brought four pounds in every week. With these I bought our food and

48

cooked with a degree of competence that I had painfully acquired to boost the talents Mother lacked. I also found the courage to bring my father up to date. He wrote back: 'That sounds wonderful,' and promised me ten pounds a month for as long as I had need. The letter left me jubilant. Into my topsy-turvy heart, the father of my early dreams had come back with a single leap to occupy the empty throne from which my rage had banished him after he left me for the girls in black.

Now with Father on 'my side', my 'dangerous' mother seemed outflanked. If 'the witch' had cut me off, hoping I would 'starve and die' just because 'I was in love', then Father and ten pounds a month would undercut her deadly plans. Uplifted by this stroke of luck, I hurled my frantic energies into pursuing the gigantic star of my prince's hopes and dreams. Without a penny to his name and parents who had both just died in a concentration camp, as the Red Cross wrote to us, his next ambition on the list was to study medicine. It did not cross his mind to join the Allied Forces, now to fight against his parents' murderers. He wished to study medicine, and his every wish was my command. My father had a wise old friend, who lived alone in Campden Hill in a noble Georgian house, high over London, deep in trees.

'Come in, my child,' he said. 'Come in.'

I left my bicycle outside and did as my protector bade.

'Delia is going to give us lunch.'

And Delia presently appeared to fulfil the prophesy.

After she had cleared away and the smoke of a cigar had blissfully enfolded me, I sank back in an old armchair and knew with absolute relief that I had come to the right door. He promised to arrange a loan. It would have to be repaid, but there would be no interest.

With such riches on the way we married and then took the train to Scotland's distant capital. There, my husband had obtained a crucial place at Surgeon's Hall. That maze of dark stone corridors, pungent with formaldehyde, in which the bodies that were destined for the dissecting room were preserved; a pile of stone, bare wooden floors, too few toilets, sinks, cold taps – there was, they reckoned, just no way to bring this dubious monument with its chequered history into the twentieth century. Certainly, throughout the war, the place hummed with activity and turned some first-rate doctors out, regardless of its gloom and stench, its cold and grim interiors, and the squalor in which traditionally many of its students lived.

My husband's road ahead seemed clear. What was I myself to do in Edinburgh for five years? The loan was just enough for one. In any case, I wished to work. The jobs I ran through all bored me stiff. The rigmarole of nine-to-five. The drab routine, the stuffy boss. Who did these people think they were, that they should order me around? Did I not have intelligence? Did I not have what it would take? And did I not already have my Part One of a BSc which entitled me to claim exemption from the First MB which prospective doctors have to pass?

I gathered all my courage up and knocked on the dark office door. The old Dean offered me a place, provided I could pay the fees. The office he had held through impecunious decades, north of the border, had instilled its own set of priorities. My mother weighed the matter up. I do not think that she believed I had it in me; nonetheless, the project merited support. Yes, she would provide the fees and, furthermore, one pound per week. But even with my father's ten, which he sent every month, the budget still fell somewhat short of minimal requirements. A further problem had been posed. I had a place, I had the fees, I was so very nearly there; once again, the rest seemed up to me. And so we rented a whole house and offered fellow students 'digs'. Through five whole years I would provide breakfast and an evening meal, full board at weekends, in the style of Edinburgh landladies, and at the same time take the course, theoretical and clinical, and sit the arduous exams. The whole heroic enterprise seemed my solitary responsibility, to my naïve, unsteady eyes.

The wartime academic year was a matter of four terms and only skimpy holidays. Medical students were 'exempt' from National Service but obliged to qualify without delay. Without knowing it, I faced a veritable marathon, denying in my habitual way anxieties the prospect ought sensibly to have aroused.

'Whatever you may undertake, you must carry it through,' my mother's dictum raved and rang in my quailing inner ear, attuned as it was to Prussian ancestors, each time my weary spirits flagged. Pride and terror drove me on.

To be a doctor offered me escape from all the hateful jobs that I had sampled off and on. With a medical degree, one was 'somebody', after all. To doctors all the world bowed down with a measure of respect. As Doctor, Mother simply could not order me around again. As Doctor, according to my own shaky lights, I would most certainly be safe from practically all the ills that had oppressed me in the past.

But higher motives also ran, akin to genuine ideals. Perhaps a doctor at her best might be like Nanny – good and kind. Perhaps, as a doctor, I would learn to comfort some forsaken child, or help another who had been abandoned, by the world at large, with hungry children on her hands. Who knows, perhaps I even hoped, in some compartment of the mind, that as a doctor I would find what ailed the stricken part of me and the means to put it right, in secret, needing no one else.

So, weighted down with shopping bags, laundry parcels, ration cards, all dragged to the dissecting room, through long lectures and endless wards, angry, weary and bemused, I somehow stumbled through the course to emerge in 1948, by what seemed a miracle, with a medical degree.

Despite such a triumphant end, the price exacted nonetheless proved to be a heavy one. The double burden took its toll of energies I had to spare. Doubtless I was anything but amusing company. Instead of carrying his share, my husband presently began looking elsewhere, now and then, to my incredulous dismay and sense of utter helplessness.

Despite opposing evidence, nothing had shaken my belief that 'he was taking care of me'. I had never lived alone. To live alone • would mean to die. How could I dare to queer his pitch without driving him away, in which case I was surely lost. This terror-stricken frame of mind left only one alternative: to ensure a substitute against the hour when I was cut off, when nourishment would be withdrawn and given to somebody else. So I responded tit for tat.

These desultory affairs were entirely meaningless. The minute he dropped his girls, I left my conquest high and dry with a huge sigh of relief. But by the time we qualified these unhappy practices had driven their enduring cracks through our marriage. This I sensed, only to deny these fears once more in the old, habitual style. And so, instead of taking stock of such a serious disarray, two doctors newly qualified, we lost precious little time in liquidating our first home and returning to the South, without delay for gratitude to Surgeon's Hall, or fond farewells.

If wartime London had welcomed us, a mother with wide open arms, by 1948 peace had started to erode that warming hospitality. The private sector was back and the busy London streets were edging out the bicycle. Rushing here and everywhere, people ran in blank pursuit of personal gain and interest in a new, hardheaded way that seemed cruelly partisan after the pally blackout ways, predicting sorrows still to come to the entire post-war world.

But neither of us had much time to waste on philosophy. With our medical degrees, won against such heavy odds, the consequent euphoria drove us, without more delay, into the hundred-hour week of house jobs we had both obtained, while neither gave the slightest thought to what this heavy load implied for our shaky partnership.

Each pocketed twelve pounds a month, after deduction for the so-called board and lodging, as those cells were named, with their narrow single beds. Our occasional weekends off did not often coincide. Under the strain of this duress, earlier cracks began to spread at a quite alarming pace. Beyond any reasonable doubt that would have been the end of that, had not a distant aunt of mine died around this very time, leaving me a legacy. These outer riches only served to overlay confusions that were incubating in our lives. They bandaged all the gaping wounds and hid them further from sight. Human chaos was infused with illusory strength and sense. Where only rubble lay before, a brand new future seemed to rise. If, a matter of hours before, we had little more than debts, the arrival of this news carried substance and some means. Like others, we could set up home, according to our own ideas.

We bought a bomb-unseated house, in something of a twilight street, but within reach of Holland Park, carrying a 'wartime grant', to remedy its tottering state. As surveyors came and went and plasterers filled in the cracks, neither of us was aware that we ourselves stood urgently in need of similar repairs and close attention. Instead, our thoughts began to turn to the dangerous cement of babies and a family.

The only babies I had ever seen lay grizzling in long rows of cots in the Edinburgh Infirmary, and belonged to something known as

'Paediatrics-for-three-months'. They had rather frightened me, those scraggy heaps of helplessness whose heads one needed to support. Parents could not visit them, because it 'only made them worse'. These 'cases' generally arrived in a most unsavoury state from 'The Haymarket', close by. This was the equivalent of Glasgow's Gorbals: grey, forbidding tenements where vermin and catastrophe scrambled mutely side by side with human failure and defeat. When these babies first arrived they came in all shades of grey of dirty washing, and the smell was equally ineffable.

Under Sister's watchful eye they were gradually restored, over the ensuing weeks, to 'bonny bairns as white as lambs', at least as far as their appearance went. If Sister had enjoyed her way, the parental banishment would have been enforced for good. They were 'nae fit to have the weens, nae for a minute', she would scold, bristling with self-righteousness. And when a baby was discharged, always as late as possible, into a pair of weary arms emitting the familiar stench, many secret tears were shed among the hard-pressed nursing staff.

If these thoughts ran through my mind, and very probably they did, adding to my unspoken fears, I never paused to search my heart whether I myself was fit to be a mother to a 'ween'. Having babies, after all, was what other people did. It seemed to be the thing to do. Besides, I tried to calm my fears, I'd manage somehow, when the time arrived, as I managed everything. Soon, I started feeling sick. My nice, firm body which had been the source of a consoling pride, became misshapen, in my eyes. And only when it seemed too late did I realize with complete dismay, that in this swollen and unappetizing state I could no longer hope to play the former game of tit for tat when my husband had affairs.

I raged at him and he raged back: 'what was wrong with an affair?' Caught, in such a frightening trap I became hysterical and filled with suicidal thoughts. There were times I wanted to throw myself beneath a car. At other times I would forget the over-whelming miseries, walk a little in the sun, and feel, inside my abdomen, some fluttering as though a bird were stirring gently in the hand. I would have liked to take it out and have a peep and put it back. Perhaps I even envied it for such a snug, warm resting place I must have coveted for myself, to hide in from a hurtful world.

Every month I went to see the local midwife who would come when I had to send for her. The uniform this lady wore was like my Nanny's, blue and white. I did not know it, at the time, but I drew comfort from this fact. The thought of her allayed my fears. I may have been a doctor, but just beneath this thin veneer lurked a tribal mother's fears and many more additional ones. Doctors and a hospital I did my utmost to avoid. Everything I had seen during the obstetrics course had merely multiplied my fears: cold, gleaming instruments; syringes, episiotomies, masks, hands in rubber gloves, being shaved and having enemas – all stirred up my paranoia to such an intolerable degree that I could have none of that.

So just before the wintry dawn of a late November day, at home in my familiar bed, I gave birth to my first child. So easily did she arrive that there was not even time to ring the midwife. In his pyjamas, half asleep, my husband caught her as she slipped from her warm and liquid world. Within two hours of her birth, the midwife had cleaned up and gone, my husband had left for work and we two were tucked up and alone, as it seemed, in the world.

I was aware of dangers like delayed post-partum haemmorhage. Part of me knew that it was mad to lie in bed, at home, alone, so shortly after giving birth. But I was even more afraid of asking anyone for help. My confounded mind proclaimed, 'You must manage things alone, to ask for help is bad and weak.' And since I simply could not ask, I stifled all reasonable fears until they somehow went away. Nature, for her part, ensures that organisms procreate only when they are mature. But in the human race we find that by giving us a mind, evolution has produced criteria for maturity that can elude her watchful eye by their vast complexity. In my case, certainly, it was an infant who had given birth. Or at least the infant part of me was still in the ascendancy over a more adult part that had not found its chance to grow into a functional entity.

In the past I had survived as adult infants generally do, by dividing my life between a cold reality and a glowing land of make-believe where everything that fantasy and wish-fulfilment could devise seemed entirely possible, into which I constantly withdrew to dream the chilly hours away. Provided that I could commute in this manner, and at will, things went tolerably well.

But now my baby's needs and cries reached me in the deepest night and in my furthest land of dreams while I wandered there by day. It seemed she left me no escape. I grew resentful and perplexed and very angry, frequently not knowing either how or why: had I not actually wanted her? In my baffled state I felt I had no minute for myself. All my impulses were subjugated to the needs of this squalling little heap that gave nothing in return. I might have grown quite violent and turned into a batterer, but fortunately I did not; some deep, enduring memory of Nanny's long and loving care must have surfaced each time my frightful loneliness drove me towards the brink.

My mother visited me once, when the baby was six weeks old. When she arrived I gave her lunch, then felt embarrassed as she watched me in this new, unsteady role. Needless to say, my milk 'dried up' in the first or second week. Doubtless there were fantasies that I was going to be sucked dry, or even, maybe, eaten up. But I was not in touch with these. Instead, and with a huge relief, I bought some bottles, several teats, Milton to sterilize them in and endless tins of powdered milk that were labelled 'national dried'. My mother watched the baby being fed. I had no way of knowing if she really truly liked the child, for she never once picked her up or kissed and cuddled her at all. Soon after coffee she got up and said she had enjoyed the lunch, but it was time to catch the train to be sure of reaching home before the rush hour began.

So winter passed and spring returned. Soon the birds began to sing before the early-morning feed. I felt that I had company. No longer did it seem that I was the only being awake when all the world lay sleeping safely within oblivion's arms. A certain sense of reprieve lightened my dark inner days. But before the tulips had unfolded to a warmer sun I was pregnant once again. And when my second daughter came, less than thirteen months had passed since the first one had arrived.

As is frequently the case, this bouncing happy little child reflected a growing confidence I must have found, despite myself, in some innermost recess. Maybe it was rooted in the sheer amazement that we all three had survived to tell the tale despite the added heartache of my husband's infidelities. Perhaps I realized I had hit rock bottom through those wintry nights and must be due to surface if only somebody would lend even half a helping hand.

In my deepest of hearts a fantasy was taking shape that I might, after all, be worth a better caretaker than I had suffered up to date.

This sense of suffering had finally started to accumulate. I was no longer, it would seem, having to get rid of it as much as previously. Experience had slowly dawned, and consequently memories tinged with that experience could gradually be built up. Once I allowed myself memories of pain, I could detect laws of cause and effect. My real lessons must have been learnt during the pregnancies, when I had no option but to suffer anguish and sit tight because there was nowhere to run, since the foundation Nanny laid had prevented the ultimate collapse that would otherwise have led to the mental hospital. But these intimations were not yet able to support a sense of my autonomy. And therefore bettering my state still meant that I must go out and find someone gentle, good and kind who was prepared to care for me and my two little ones. Someone who would stay with me and not keep having other girls. Someone who would understand that I really needed this kindness and a second chance, however vague the project seemed.

As these new longings took on shape they were magically personified in a lover who would wish me well – while I realized that I had a profession up my sleeve and some money in the bank. In other words, a certain sense that some value might just possibly attach to me now dawned in this symbolic manner after the battering received by two successive pregnancies and in the total absence of supportive, genuine concern. And as the sap of summer rose so did this feeling germinate that I deserved a better fate, though it was still too deeply buried to find its way to consciousness – except by being acted out.

This play consisted of three acts. I found myself a part-time job as assistant to a young GP whose practice was not far away, and also bought a little car, which I clearly needed for this work. With my salary I could then pay for a 'mother's help', to look after 'all the rest'. Finally I got down to the fundamental quest: for someone to take care of me. Through the months I scrutinized every single man I met to see if he might be the one to save me from a marriage that now seemed totally iniquitous. Once or twice I tried them out in a flimsy love affair.

None of these men showed any signs of wanting me and two

small girls, so I in turn cold-shouldered them, for falling lamentably short of the substance of my dream. Undeterred the search went on, until one day I found a boy who really fell in love with me, as I believed I had with him. An Indian student, wholly without means, he offered with grave certainty to lead me to my promised land.

The better course would certainly have been to find a tough solicitor and let him handle everything. For, once my husband understood that I was planning to leave him, he started playing on my fears and deepest insecurities. What judge in his right mind, he jibed, would let a whore have custody? Right, so I had better stay around, fulfil my duties as a wife and thank my lucky stars each night that in the kindness of his heart he was still putting up with me.

Reeling with a sense of shame, it seemed to me he must be right; the law would wash its hands of me. Not once did it occur to me that he was speaking from inside a larger glass-house than my own. Besides, I felt too terrified, for as he came to recognize that I had found somebody else he became violent, and still it did not dawn on me, even after some awful beatings up, that in the light of these events the courts might step in on my side. Instead, I limped out of his life, my right leg in a plastercast, determined in my woolly mind that I would get my little ones by hook or by crook, even though by now my husband was a consultant psychiatrist.

But if there was no going back, where did 'forward' lie? 'My parents will look after you, in Calcutta,' said the boy. 'Ma loves children. You will see. I will follow in a year and everything will be alright.'

I started dreaming day and night of this warm and distant land, where parents were awaiting me who loved small girls and would be kind and take care of everything under starry, Indian skies to the rustle of the palms. Accordingly I made my plans. While my husband was at work, I pleaded with the German girl to let me take my daughters out, just for an hour, just for once. Before the hour was up we were, all three of us, high in the air, on our way to Italy. From Genoa we would take a boat to India and a new life.

But those who live in dreamland will be ousted by reality. On our small Italian beach, where only local children played, out of clear Italian skies and surrounded by blue uniforms my husband suddenly appeared, followed by a straggling mob of reporters weighted down with greedy cameras, racing over empty sands like some wild, pedestrian hunt on the scent of us – their prey. Interpol had done its job.

'Either give the children up or face prison for contempt of court,' this large male chorus bayed and waved sheets of paper that carried an intimidating seal at the only female in this tragi-comic opera scene. I stood before them all alone, in no more than a bathing suit, while a dozen cameras clicked.

It appeared I had no choice. They offered me a final night together with my little ones in the room we had obtained from a local fisherman. The next day in a cloud of dust an impressive motorcade carried both of them away. With a flourish and a bow and a final click of heels my passport was restored to me and the little sunsoaked stage reverted to obscurity.

Back in London, once again, I had at long last to admit that the law was now my final hope – old gentlemen in wigs and gowns, frozen with self-righteousness, who spat on outcasts like myself. Behind a brass plate, up three floors, in a veritable maze of dark and draughty corridors which led to countless little rooms, I tracked down a solicitor. I told him everything I knew relating to those ten, bleak years, and watched the gentleman turn pale. With his silvery-grey hair, dark suit and gleaming white starch, doubtless he had never seen the like of me for sheer depravity. After an eternity, he raised his head:

'The latest is an Indian, yes? We'll have to lose that gentleman. And you will have to buy a house. You see,' he glanced at sheets of notes with a gesture of despair, 'the judge will have to be convinced that you are . . . hmm, respectable.' He gave a deep, alarming sigh, asked for two hundred pounds in advance and promised he would do his best provided that I now obeyed all instructions faithfully.

'Even if it breaks my heart?' I asked my mentor tearfully.

'You have no alternative,' spoke the oracle again. 'Young lady, from this hour on you are innocence personified.' His eyes were feasting on my breasts. He gave a comic little shrug and rang a charming silver bell. The secretary showed me out with a dark, contemptuous glare.

I had never lived alone before in my entire life. The prospect frightened me to death. But as the divorce machinery ground into the malignant stride of a huge, contested case, I knew that I was being watched by what was called 'the other side'.

This term lent fearful overtones to my terrors, day and night. Tearfully I parted from the Indian boy, my only friend. I took a small bedsitting-room with a tiny kitchenette, in which I would sit out this siege while I tried to buy a house. Sometimes, after it was dark, I thought I saw a little man on the pavement opposite. I thought I saw him now and then as I went about my life. I grew more and more confused. What was this evidence he sought? Was he watching me the way mother watched me, when I ate, to check my table etiquette? Was he watching what I wrote, what I wore and what I read? My life seemed such a total mess, as I saw it through his eyes, still projecting everything. My life, as I now studied it from this stranger's point of view, seemed tospy-turvy, upside-down, not worthy of the name of A Life. I felt certain that he thought it was high time I tackled it in some fundamental way.

Exactly what did he expect? What was it that I ought to do in order to set his mind at rest that I could prove to be a mother to my two little ones, that I could lead a wholesome life if only someone showed me how. Just how the whole idea took root, I am no longer certain, but the detective's watchful eye, that mobilized my paranoia, unquestionably played a part in deciding me to seek for some far-reaching help; for without it, I was lost. The proof lay in that little man on the pavement opposite my lonely window, dusk after dusk.

To realize that I needed help was, of course, all very well, but what kind of help and from whom? I had seen enough of psychiatry to feel that I would sooner jump off London Bridge than seek help from those who walked the grim asylum corridors with bunches of jangling keys. Besides, I rather thought I saw a gleam of madness in their eyes. As a student I had felt that patient and psychiatrist seemed somehow interchangeable, nor did my husband give me cause to doubt my intuition there. That the twentieth century offered an alternative, I had no inkling of. The medical curriculum, then, as now, did not expect that future doctors should need to be aware of something as obscure – as totally irrelevant – as the discoveries of Freud.

Jung was another matter, though. In the early fifties Jung was something of a household name with the mystically inclined; those who ten years later walked the airy 'flower-children' path. Jung was gentle, kind and wise. I had come across his book, *Modern Man in Search of a Soul*. That was certainly myself. At this hour of my need it rang a loud and noble bell through the valleys of my mind. And so one morning I set out from my small bedsitting-room to go in search of help from Jung. I thought perhaps the little man would approve of such a step.

My Jungian Mother

High on a rising Hampstead hill, on a sunny autumn day, the Jungian doctor gazed at me through his horn-rimmed spectacles. He had taken many notes and looked tired now, I thought. The silence in the carefully tended room was ticking like a metronome. My mind lost interest and skipped into the garden, down below, where the yellow roses drooped. It seemed a lovely place to play and shake off the endless worries that were always dogging me.

'Doctor, alright, I will write to you,' his voice came and dragged me back again.

'I would like a lady though . . . that is, if you do not mind.'

'I agree with you,' he smiled, 'I was thinking that myself. Now then, let me show you out.'

I cast a final, yearning look at the garden where I would never be allowed to play, as the doctor's children could, and then my battered little Ford took me back to Kensington, and the conditions of my siege.

At long last the letter came. I went at the appointed hour with a sense of gnawing fear that seemed a little ludicrous. 'Silly child, you won't be hurt,' I kept repeating out aloud, as though addressing someone else. 'You are going to sit nice and still and have some psychotherapy and I am going to find the means.'

It felt as though the one addressed was struggling hard to get away as I rang the front-door bell of a pretty little house in a dreamy Mayfair street, redolent with little shops which have long since fallen to the axe of the developers. A motherly, small personage in a vaguely eastern dress bade me follow her upstairs. Ageless, timeless, effortless, she floated up ahead of me. Everything about her seemed elusive, yet entirely real, enchanting and yet business-like. Two chairs were standing face to face among

61

the many books and plants that were thriving everywhere; they seemed to dominate the room, as an altar does a church. I felt that God was watching us, or maybe it was really Jung. Could the two possibly be one, I asked myself uncertainly.

What did she expect of me, this lady with the gentle smile? It seemed she wanted me to come and see her three times every week. Her fee, she said, would be three pounds. The times were such and such she read from an impressive diary and she was glad that I had come. Presently, I found myself on the pavement once again. A smell of bonfires from the nearby park was drifting through the sunny streets, among the little cottages, in one of which I had just sat, before being promptly ejected back into the outer world of cars and bonfires, men and trees. It all seemed somehow like a dream, but still the desperate sense of fear was tugging wildly at my sleeve: a child all set to run away, although I had no child with me, I pondered, feeling very sad. It was as though I sensed how long a journey lay ahead, through weeks and months and even years. What skill and patience it would take to bring me out of Dreamland, which we call a narcissistic state, to learn to face the outer world on its terms and not my own.

I had to find nine pounds a week for the psychotherapy and something like another ten to cover rent and food and car. I obtained a new assistantship in the heart of Shepherd's Bush. It paid enough to meet these needs. But more than that, I liked the work. Helping others, who were sick, offered me a sense of worth, an inkling of identity. A doctor could not be as bad as I very often felt, especially after visiting the high-minded solicitor, compiling affidavits of everything that had gone on between my husband and myself. These files were growing by the week. Every single page was sworn. Builders, plumbers, charladies, all, he claimed, were witnesses to faithlessness and violence, all manner of monstrosities. I often felt he went too far. Had my husband and myself really been as bad as that? There were moments when I felt I wanted to come to his defence.

'Well, was your leg, or was it not, in plaster Doctor, when you left?'

'Of course it was, but even so . . .'

'Young lady, there can be no "buts" when you stand before the judge.'

Alice in Wonderland that I was, this legal world of black and white, shrinking and growing by turns, took some beating; nonetheless, since I had no alternative, I tagged along and acquiesced in what seemed like one more aspect of life's bewildering masquerade.

Meanwhile, I had found a house that instantly enchanted me. The sellers, who were Catholics, were moving nearer to their church and within easy reach of early-morning mass. A buoyant, close-knit family, their lively, warm responsiveness seemed to infuse the very bricks and go together with the house, as did the tall trees both front and back where large communal gardens lay that any child was bound to love. It all seemed like a dream come true. If most of it must be let off to pay the awesome mortgage back, this seemed a small price to pay for owning this gracious, terraced house, so different in its ambience from the one that I had fled, whose very memory made me cry. The trouble was that I thought I had to hide these tears from V, my Jungian analyst.

Three times a week I went along and sat obediently in her chair, because, it seemed, she wanted that. I intended to do everything exactly as she wished and be no trouble. It was kind of her to let me come, considering how bad I was, the awful things that I had done. I only hoped that I could hide the wicked thoughts that crossed my mind the very minute I sat down. Since I hid these from myself as thoroughly as possible, as is generally the case with a badly scuttled mind, I could not even pin them down. They were certainly concerned with feelings both of love and hate that I was experiencing towards V, feelings as old as I myself, manoeuvring somewhere in the dark to have an airing at long last. Here was their opportunity. But Jung was never much concerned with the infant struggling to get out in the course of psychotherapy. His genius overlooked this fundamental ABC, which it scorned as 'reductive', in its search for higher truths and transcendental nourishment. This the infantile mind cannot digest or utilize, where it has failed to solve its earlier conflict situations. So all this turmoil remained angrily under lock and key for another two decades.

I still remember my first dream. I was running naked through a field where thistles and dark nettles tore at my body to the chin. There was a cowshed where I hoped to find something good and warm, but the cows were hanging from the ceiling, hopelessly out of reach. I felt cheated and afraid.

How well the dream depicts the plight of one who suffers from self-destructive impulses. With how much clarity it shows how everything good and nourishing is experienced as being beyond reach, without any hope that this predicament might change. It conjures up complete despair, an utter depth of hopelessness. But why was the maternal milk suspended there, so, so far away? Had I put it out of reach of some greedy baby-self for fear of gobbling it all and possibly the breast itself? Did I feel guiltily that it belonged to a baby brother once that baby brother had been born? Did I see my analyst as a bad, withholding mother? Had I turned her into one out of envy, greed or spite? In other words, what part had my own destructive impulses actually been playing here? The Jungian cosmology seemed to be above such matters as a baby and her milk. True, there was the archetype of the 'Great Mother'. There she loomed, the Virgin and the Courtesan, Kali, the Destroying Witch, the Feeding Mother of the milk and corn. Vast, majestic, there she stood, reconciling opposites within a great revolving whole.

Jung would have argued forcefully that these awe-inspiring symbols, old as mankind itself, will integrate those polarities in the mind whereby experience is split into 'good' and 'bad', as into black and white. But he did not acknowledge how the baby's own omnipotence will constitute the archetype in every single given case. For this reason, I believe, it is open to debate whether the gravely damaged mind can ever be susceptible to any adequate degree to this approach: 'the Shadow' and 'the Persona', 'the Human Types' and 'the Mandala'; these constitute a luxury. But the sick and starving mind gasps for deeper understanding the infant can assimilate.

For weeks and months, for eight whole years, we wandered through these august realms whose subtle wisdom could not touch the whirling fragments of my dislocated mind. It was like bringing an untrammelled child, reared among shrieking ghosts and blood-stained effigies of voodoo, into a fine, Byzantine church to further its education and end up totally confused. As the weeks and months ran by we seemed like two anthropologists engaged on some gigantic dig, with the growing probability that neither of us would re-emerge from the trenches of myth into the light of day, that had long since been left behind.

I had little inkling of the subterfuges of the schizoid mind, its frenzied need to withdraw from contact to some hiding place in an idyllic world of dreams; its rages and hostilities when its cravings are not met by an idealized response, and its terror of the need for love. And she was simply not equipped, by the 'Zürich' school of Jung, rooted in metaphysics rather than in child psychology, for this long drawn-out pursuit of a chilly fish that slips the net and must be constantly retrieved if any healing is to take place. So she embellished for me, year by year, the exquisite Jungian tapestry of mandalas and archetypes, that ultimately promised land which I myself would never reach.

Enchanting as these issues seem when depicted in the works of Jung, helpful as they would seem to be to others who are seeking help and whose difficulties are possibly less primitive, the conflicts in my deeper mind were never really reached or touched, even if, as we shall see, there were accidental gains which would save a later day.

After I had been with V some fifteen months, the solicitors had at last drawn their battle lines. A day for the hearing was agreed. But as I waited in the court, shaking with fear and quite alone, a sudden ripple seemed to run through the segregated camps of the exponents of the law.

'You may go home. Our case is won,' my solicitor announced, as he steered me to one side.

My several witnesses had all been 'interfered with', he explained, with satisfaction in his voice, 'which constitutes a felony, should the gentleman persist'. He spoke of vindication now, as one who had never for a moment been in doubt; but I was simply overcome and numb with terror at these words. They only proved I was no match for the sorrows that were still to come from a man who, I now knew, would not stop at anything.

And so, indeed, it soon turned out.

'Daddy says you're horrible for taking us away from him. He says he'll die from missing us. You left him. Daddy says you're bad, and Daddy knows he's going to die.' And weekly access reinforced these diabolic messages.

'Get me evidence and I will have access stopped that very day,' thundered the solicitor.

But how could I get 'evidence'? Neither of the children ate and nightmares woke them from their sleep. 'Daddy's going to die,' they sobbed, in answer to my questioning.

Fragmented being that I was, lacking all inner and all outer props, this seemed more than I could bear. Day after day and night after night, the three of us were quite alone in the enormous, empty house that was hardly yet a home. Rooms stood empty, floorboards creaked, uncurtained windows seemed to glare, naked light-bulbs shed a hard and uncompromising light.

Neither could I think of V, my only contact with the outside world, as someone who was on my side. The members of my family had for the most part steered well clear of my scandalous affairs, and I had no experience yet of a love that stays the course, however rough the going gets. True, in those parts of my mind that Nanny had infused with light, I sensed that such a love exists, as the early dream had shown, but placed far beyond my reach, not to be interpreted for another twenty years.

If everyone had gone away, instead of rallying around, when I needed their support, why should V be different? She must be angry with me now, for making such a mess of things in my hour of victory. She would scold me cruelly and maybe even punish me, as my mother used to do if I disappointed her. Accordingly, I went along like an obedient little girl, and sat dumbfounded, almost mute, hoping that the time would pass and we need not go into things too closely, until another day, which was then postponed in turn; while V had simply no idea how to get onto my track as I absconded more and more, despite the attendance that some part of me put in religiously.

My main anxiety, that I had nothing good at all to offer my two little ones, or her, or anyone on earth, was never once taken up. That the psychotic mind, with its destructive impulses, is filled with dread on that account, and keeps all others at arm's length – often for their own protection – V did not understand.

Isolated from the world, under all this stress and strain, both the children and I promptly started to fall ill, converting blind anxiety into mysterious temperatures, vomiting and diarrhoea. The house became a stricken place, to which my former husband found access very readily, and within six or seven weeks he had both children back with him where they seemed happy, ate and slept, so that I 'could not find the heart' to let this tug of war go on. This was how I idealized my own collusion in this sorry deed. In truth I lacked all inner strength to fight this lonely war on every frontier of my life, without that essential topping up of self-esteem which spurious relationships could not supply; I had become an addict.

Wanting above everything 'to do my very best for them', as I glibly told myself, I took a blind and short-term view promising a quick way out and agreed to let the court nullify my hard-won gains to leave my daughters in those hands that left so much to be desired. Then, with a sigh of deep relief, my shallow, stray-cat heart resumed its preoccupation with finding that elusive prince who would take care of me, now that the solicitor's looming shadow was thankfully withdrawn. And so my thoughts turned to the man and to the notion of some perfect love which had cheated me so far. That my needs for love were still those of an infant at the breast, wanting nourishment and warmth and very little else besides, I had no means of knowing then. Nor that the analysis, had it taken proper root, should have satisfied those needs for the time being, certainly. Relieved of all the harsh constraints which the legal battle had imposed, after all these lonely months I set sail once more for 'love', that perilous commodity I always saw a haven in, rather than an honest workshop to adapt throughout our life.

Three months before, I now recalled, a mutual friend had taken me to meet a memorable man, in his Hampstead studio. And now my memory returned, almost pristine, to that hour. The day had hardly awoken yet for all of us were early birds. At a mast-like easel stood a man, fixed like a captain to his bridge, wrapped thickly in a dressing gown, that must at one time have been brown. He was entirely absorbed, as little children at their play, and though he signalled to us be at home, remained oblivious and alone. So, I had found myself at ease to take such new surroundings in, as I had never seen before. The light and lofty studio space simply took my breath away. A tree in blossom and in fruit, it harboured treasures that had come from the four ends of the earth, in careless, masterful array. Through lofty glass the sky loomed overhead, bright as the polar hunting grounds. Through further glass towards the north, a tangled, wintry garden pressed its nose against the frosty panes, while a cast-iron studio stove, ample-bellied as a whale, emitted an enormous warmth. At least, I thought it was the stove.

Eventually the man paused from his work and introductions could take place. But it was all too evident the artist's mind stuck to his work and used the small talk as a knack to keep the outer world at bay. Presently, without ado, he pulled some shabby corduroys over pink pyjama pants and added a brown daytime smock. But never once, while part of him was doing this or doing that, or casting quick, expressive talk, was one deceived that he had been distracted from the inner glance fixed on the canvas he was working on. It evidently was his all, as he caressed it here and there by adding pigment with his brush, then, taking a few quick steps back, surveyed it, head cocked to one side, as will a lover his beloved. Forward and back and to and fro, he moved for it and it alone. It seemed that I was witnessing a sequence from a mystic's dance. A dedication to the source with which no other could compete or ever hope to be compared. The whole experience was a dream I knew I had always longed to emulate in my own life. And now the time had come for this Polish painter and myself to meet again, a second time.

'Do you still remember me,' I quavered on the telephone with my usual diffidence.

'Forget a beautiful girl like you? You'll be my model. Come along this afternoon, let's say at four because I'm busy later on.'

This brief communiqué contained a forecast of the perplexities I was soon to be entangled in, personified in this one man: sudden, all-embracing warmth, followed by complete withdrawal, when contact seemed too dangerous.

J welcomed me with open arms and beatific radiance. He offered me some tea and cake from a tiny kitchenette where Polish bread and sauerkraut and gherkins all lay side by side, a delicatessen in miniature, then said 'Alright, you can undress and put your clothes onto my bed.' His tone of voice was business-like and I took my cue from that, always more than willing to let someone else be in command. 'Stand over there, or walk about. You're very beautiful,' he said, in that voice which offered warmth, only to take it all straight back in that baffling way of his of alternating hot and cold, I had already learned to dread.

After an hour of intensive work, in the course of which I felt stripped to the impersonal, like a landscape or still-life, he said, 'Alright, put on your clothes. At six o'clock I'm going out. You've got some minutes first, to rest. Sit down, girl, and be comfortable.' I did exactly as he said. More than gladly I had signed my little scrap of life away into his keeping there and then, eager to be rid of it – the whole responsibility, which I felt as such a heavy drag. Yet, at the same time I felt sad, as if acknowledging a loss I could not put a finger on.

'Look, next time we'll go out and eat,' he offered warmly, 'afterwards'. I was instantly disarmed. Every little show of warmth bought a particle of me that hungered for it so much. At six precisely we both left. Taking brisk, decisive steps he moved at an impressive pace for a man who was quite short, and yet looked massive, nonetheless, in his shapeless, flapping clothes: brown corduroy and navy serge, the oddest mixture in my eyes; and yet, somehow it suited him – haphazards, welded into one.

So he walked east and I drove west feeling thoroughly confused. Was this a beginning or an end? What on earth, for goodness sake, had hit me this time round, and where? What was one to make of it? I quickly pushed these thoughts away. It was not my habit to ask such questions of myself. I preferred the blindfold leap in the maximum of dark. Within a few days I was back and it was the same routine, except that he kept his word. I cannot say he took me out, but with him when he went to eat. I got the feeling one must eat and sleep – if one is going to work. And in this way he took me back – to sleep with him, in a swaying single bed under layers of African tribal blankets, black and red. I felt like some great chief's concubine.

Enchanted, puzzled and perplexed, I lay awake for a long time, gazing at the summer night through great skylights, overhead, feeling curiously at peace and at the same time frozen scared, exposed to some appalling risk I could not understand. That I had merged my life into his, keeping nothing for myself, I had no inkling of, as yet. Only much later would I learn how to extricate myself, once I had been helped to build foundations to support me as a clearly defined entity with its own, true boundaries.

I awoke to find I had the little bed all to myself. The glass around me was still dark, which at midsummer meant that it was barely four o'clock. Nothing moved and nothing stirred. Then I saw a pool of light, at the studio's furthest end, and in its circle glowed the man, again, in that brown dressing gown, seated with his back to me – drawing – lost to all the world.

Slowly, the first birds awoke. Light came from a wider source through the great expanse of glass, and far away the traffic of London growled gearing up for work. The man remained oblivious. It seemed to be up to me to guard whatever was between us now, until he too returned to it – assuming that he wanted to, for I could not believe he would. In a trance-like state I dressed, washed a little at the sink, made the funny, throne-like bed, with its many different layers rather like a baby's cot, and tip-toed up the wooden stairs.

'I'll be ringing you. OK?' Long before I found my voice to formulate some sweet response, he had returned to regions to which I sensed I had no access, neither claim nor right. But claim or no claim, I would fight, if need be, the entire world to make this entrancing man let me keep him for myself.

These events took place in an analytic break that had lasted several months, for V had meanwhile fallen ill. When the analysis resumed I discovered she had moved from Mayfair to a little flat at the back of Marble Arch. I dared not comment on all this. The implications were too big in 'Oedipal' and other terms; nor did they get analysed in this Jungian no-man's-land, devoid of any 'transference', so that my deep anxieties only multiplied apace. But V, in fact, had just split up, as she told me later on when we had become good friends, with a gifted and impetuous man whose preoccupations had proved too difficult for her.

V and J, it now turned out, had formerly been distant friends. When she heard of my affair and who this lovely artist was, V determined I should not have to suffer her own fate. Artists were all very well at their easel, but nowhere else. Forgetting or ignoring that analysts should analyse unconscious content, neither more nor less, and, to use Bion's well-known phrase, should 'eschew memory and desire', V overstepped these boundaries. She made no bones about the fact that she was averse to my new relationship. Women needed husbands, not the tantrums of a genius. They required a measure of support for their growth and happiness which such a man could not supply, overburdened as he was by his creative incubus. She clearly did not trust me to make the right choice for myself, once I was clear about my need, and after we had analysed the deeper conflicts thoroughly. Part of me bowed down to this and agreed emphatically. Attention-seeking child that I was, how could I accept the fact that painting was J's 'foremost love', and in my insecurity it seemed that he must choose between his work and woman-love, since that work excluded me as all creative intercourse excludes the 'other'. But a more rebellious part of my personality fought her view, quite convinced that V grudged me every happiness, above all in the sexual sphere, since we had not analysed the envious mother in my inner world. Her interventions made me feel that these transference fantasies were grounded in reality, which only multiplied my suspicions and hostility.

My only happy times with J seemed to be when we spent an afternoon together, somewhere in the open air; or a weekend now and then, exploring countryside or coast, far from that hateful studio. On those occasions I felt I 'had won', and my triumph knew no bounds. Every other day he worked from dawn to sunset, round the clock, seven days of the week! He even worked on Christmas Day, to my absolute disgust. Only when the evening came would he, once or twice a week, spare me any time at all. And even that was limited to the arrival of the dawn.

On certain evenings he taught, on others he visited his wife, from whom I knew he lived apart, hoping that she would in time agree to give him a divorce. But my possessiveness was such that I had little sympathy for his feelings of concern for her precarious state of mind. She too was in analysis, and J was quite determined to let the legal questions ride until she found her feet again, while I was far too clamorous to recognize that he was right.

All of this was fuel to the little fires that V still stoked, instead of helping me to see that the roots of my hostility lay in feeling overlooked, and not at the centre of life's stage at every moment of the day or night. So in our sessions we meandered, week by week, through every sort of archetype, 'the Hero', 'the Wise Old Man', 'the Virgin Mother' . . . everything except the rages in my heart that I was not in full control of everything in poor J's life. These rages I drew no nearer to understanding as time passed; and so another year went by.

But if J and I had our differences that darkened far too many hours, we had our sunny days as well, as love was slowly taking root despite my shallow, stony soil. Our evenings frequently began with carefree strolls through London's parks in their fine variety, and dawn would find us by the Thames at Battersea or Hammersmith or Dockland, down in the East End, watching the river's murky tide play with its assorted toys of bottles, driftwood, cork and cans. On winter mornings I would rise at his hour of four or five and drive him to the studio he was clearly pining for from the moment he awoke. Both of us were pretty broke at that moment in our lives, and taxis, used as a routine, were totally beyond our means. J refused to share my house, since it lacked a studio. A studio he had to have. No ordinary room would do.

'It has no workshop atmosphere. I've always lived in studios.' For J, a house seemed like a trap.

But there was more to it than that. J was simply terrified of a close relationship in case it broke again. Neither could he contemplate the responsibility.

'My father was a broken man,' he would frequently repeat, a note of warning in his voice. 'He could not feed his family. My mother worked her fingers to the bone taking people's washing in. We were eight people in a room.'

'But everything is different now,' I would answer tearfully, feeling rejected and unloved, behind which lurked my buried fear of real responsibility.

'I am a painter,' he would growl. 'Leave me out of all your plans. Go, find yourself a nice, young man, who has time for all these things like houses and a family.'

And listening to these words of his, repeated in a weary voice, week by week and month by month, I failed to tune into their tone which was a very different one: 'If only it were possible. If only I could have a home. If only I could have a child and the inner certainty that I could provide for it everything a child should have, instead of hunger and pogroms, the privations that I knew and would not wish on anyone . . .' But through my scolding and my tears, nonetheless, some part of me responded deeply to that plangent song, that echoed loud and clear my own longings for a child – for after eighteen months had passed I knew I was expecting one.

There was no hope of J's divorce, and V felt very dubious whether I was strong enough to go through the ordeal of unmarried motherhood which, in the middle fifties, was still an onerous affair, fraught with scandal of all sorts and wearisome unpleasantness.

'But I have a house,' I said, 'and I will put a brass plate up and start a practice of my own. Who can stop me. Tell me that?'

Holland Park at the time was still a so-called 'Medium Zone' in the National Health Service. This meant that any doctor could get permission to start up in general practice, even if it took considerable time to build a decent 'List' of patients if one chose to 'squat'. And as the autumn days drew on, and the leaves were glowing red and gold, and bonfires cast their incense all around that house of mine, my heart sang out, 'I have a house, I have a plate, and I am going to have a child. No one can stop me in the whole, wide world. This child is going to be mine, and no one will dare take it away.' Before this inner certainty the opposition fell away like the walls of Jericho before that fervent trumpet call.

So far, I have mainly dwelt on the inadequacies of my analysis with V, and the Jungian 'walkabout'. But if I now had confidence in 'a house' and in 'a plate', this meant that I had some belief in a wholesome inner space that was safe and good enough to let another baby grow, and in my capacity to provide for it, when born. Since such inner certainties were not in evidence before, doubtless the analysis had played a certain part in their gradual emergence now, together with support from J, intermittent though it was.

After all, I had by now been with V for two whole years, and three times a week at that. She had never let me down. I had always found her kind and even-tempered, never harsh, preoccupied or punitive, from all of which I must have drawn some image of a mother with whom I could identify. Most likely this had reinforced the earlier good experience with my Nanny, in Berlin. Perhaps V had topped it up sufficiently for me to feel this whiff of brand new confidence. Some of its components were doubtless sheer euphoria and bursts of wild omnipotence, that could have also boded ill, especially as I thrust my fears into the background of my dreams in a very manic way, wildly waving doubts aside. Nevertheless, the bubble held. I went to V three times a week, right through the pregnancy, and for two or three more years beyond. I began to trust her more and feel a measure of support which evidently just sufficed, though deeper issues lay quite neglected through these years.

Meanwhile J bestirred himself to buy a studio of his own. His Hampstead landlady refused to have any dealings with fallen women like myself. A spinster, and a bit adrift on the tides of loneliness, she never liked me at the best of times – slender and respectable. But it was very evident that she would have no truck with any baby that was born out of wedlock. Come what may, J did not buy us all a home, to my considerable grief, but nonetheless he bought a house that had a splendid studio and two empty rooms besides, which he used for storing canvases. The other six were occupied by 'sitting tenants' due to leave by the end of the decade under certain wartime laws. The purchase was a symbol of his ambivalence at the time. And even though I raged at him, I recognized the hopeful signs of progress we had clearly made, since J was obviously concerned to do the very best he could within the limits of his fear that family life endangered him.

And so the months of pregnancy ran through the winter and on to spring. Meanwhile my practice slowly grew into a means of slight support, while, totally out of the blue, my mother offered to pay for my psychotherapy till I could manage this again. The world had grown a safer place than I had ever known before. I even liked my pregnant state, for the first time in my life, because J found it beautiful. He started drawing me once more, with obvious pleasure, I could see. And though I sensed that this response came from the artist rather than the man, it reassured me nonetheless. But I still mistrusted men very deeply and steered clear of obstetricians once again until the child was overdue. Then I had to seek advice in my baby's interests. And when that turned out to be a caesarian I agreed that it be done with 'local' for the baby's sake.

When I started coming round, J was standing by the bed suffused in happiness and pride and an inner radiance I had never seen before. I realized instantaneously, that despite all earlier doubts, a father had been born as well. We agreed to call our son David, which had been the name of J's own father who had died, together with his entire family, in the Warsaw Ghetto siege. And ten days later I was back in my house in Holland Park with a baby in my arms.

It was spring. The trees were just stirring into frills of leaf, and ornamental cherry trees, splendid in their pink and white, lined the roads which the taxi took. The first night or two I wept, barely convalescent and overcome by loneliness and apprehensions in the dark. But days broke early in the spring. The birds soon kept me company, and my son was beautiful: flawless each time happiness broke through doubts and fears. Before the month was out optimism won the day to occupy the stage for good. So richly was this child endowed with gifts of natural happiness, it seemed that I drew strength from him and grew in confidence from week to week.

In those steady buoyant days I fooled myself that I had won over the darkness for all time and that the tunnel's distant light was enfolding me for good. I had no inkling that I still lacked a foundation to my life and had built on sand again; that if misfortune were to strike I was still no match for it, although the subsequent collapse still lay many years away.

I had my house, my son, a growing practice of my own, and J – who at times seemed there, at others far away again, but still drew nearer through the years. And, at the end of the decade, when his sitting tenants left and his divorce came through, at last I moved into his studio house and we were married finally. I missed my trees and Holland Park, where my heart and roots remained, but I still had my practice there in my own, beloved house, and struggled bravely to adjust to the new teeming neighbourhood, its grey brick houses and strange, scruffy ways.

V, I realized, disapproved. My Jungian analysis was, at this time, winding up.

'Nini, you are too young for that.'

'What is that supposed to mean?' I asked her with hostility.

'No dedicated artist can make a husband,' V replied. 'Artists are exceptions to every single human rule.'

These comments frightened me the more since J himself had always urged, 'Listen girl, steer clear of painters. Find yourself a nice young man who has nothing on his mind. A maharajah who can buy you lots of lovely elephants.'

'Why should I want an elephant?' I would hurl back in dismay.

But I had simply no idea what a 'husband' really was, or marriage, or a family. I had no inkling, at the time, what a real commitment could conceivably imply. Unlike a bird's, my mind still held no imprint of how to build a nest, or rear my young until they could fly. But rather than confront this lack in myself, where it belonged, I would hurl it all at J with hostility and arrogance. I thought that, if I wished, I could make anything work, regardless of reality. I left my Jungian mother's flat, carrying J's second child, baffled and a little sad, her words still ringing in my ears, wondering what lay ahead yet feeling that it must be good. I still assumed that V must grudge me every married happiness, for we had never touched upon Oedipal anxieties in this cosmology of Jung.

Our second baby was a girl. We gave her J's mother's name: Sara, whom he had loved so much and deeply, though he rarely spoke of the many-peopled world whose passions and vitality Nazi savagery had sent up as so much fuel for so little smoke. The weeks that followed on her birth should have warned me urgently that my difficulties were far from over, even yet. I felt anxious and depressed and longed to put the clock back to our earlier family of three. I feared I might not have enough to offer to this little girl, who unlike D, cried half the night, with a piercing, desperate tone that often made my blood run cold with dark forebodings and with crazy fears. Had I spent all my love on D? I dreaded he might feel deprived each time I picked the baby up, although he was five by then and I was teaching him to read, which he mastered in four weeks; a robust, easy-going child who brimmed with steadfast confidence.

Yet something in my inmost heart squealed with terror during those first weeks, so unlike the carefree ones that followed on the birth of D. Subterranean tremors shook my inner being night and day, while I did everything I could to brush those harbingers aside. Had I not 'been analysed' – dark assumption: dangerous trap! Was it not my job to know that 'mothers often get the blues'?

As the weeks ran into months the volcano settled down without eruption, and eventually it seemed that all was well again once I was safely back at work and reassured by routine, while an able 'mother's help', coped with everything at home. Lunacy had once again been bundled into a dark sack. Instead denial won the day. It focused on a fantasy that would cost us very dear: that of an idyllic home, for the perfect family. Probably my mind went back to that Bavarian still-life of my distant childhood days: a farm on green and wooded slopes. J had always wanted to leave the great city for a quieter routine in some remote, untroubled place where the seasonal pendulum dictated the main events, and the disruptions of the social scene could readily be held at bay. Besides, as many parents do, we reasoned that children should grow up in the healthy, open air, and failed to take into account that both of us were quite devoid of the protective colouring the English country-side demands from any of its would-be squires: the farming–hunting protocol, its musty Christianity and ritualistic primacy centred on the village pub; the hierarchical ballyhoo of those who, down the centuries, have owned the cottages, the land and, to all intents and purposes, the agricultural labourer.

But I of course held little truck with the trivia of reality, while J was totally immune to its tricks and vagaries provided he was left to paint the year round, undisturbed. And so my fantasy obtained carte blanche and dangerously wanton reins. After a windswept weekend on the shingle beaches of its weather-harried coasts, our sights fell on East Anglia. The light and skies wheeled marvellous. Traffic on its winding lanes seemed dreamy after London's roar, as tractors turned into a field or barn like rabbits vanish down a hole. The place slept hauntingly remote, untouched by dual carriage-ways. It bore a clear resemblance to the Flemish landscapes which J had loved in Belgium, before the war, and stirred nostalgic memories of the Flemish painters he had known. It touched my own romantic depths. And so East Anglia it was.

We found a crumbling rectory endearingly devoid of mains. Its grey brick elevations loomed grandly and forsakenly over ten acres of neglected land, three ponds and old-established trees that flanked a long, impressive drive hiding the house from common view. Neglect had gradually edged former gardens from the scene and the apple orchards dreamt in tangled silence, undisturbed but for the flutter and scamper of creatures hidden from the eye. There was a huge and leaning barn, which J claimed would make a studio. It stood some distance from the house and fronted three mysterious ponds astir with wildlife of their own. The place was going for a song, since anyone in his right mind would have steered well clear of it unless dedicated to the restoration of the past.

But, where others shook their heads, I saw a challenge. As for my husband, thankfully he left such matters in my hands not doubting they were strong enough for the most herculean task, and I projected this belief with the despairing energy that the helpless often put on show, and that others like to take on trust if it serves their interests. Consequently, under my command, a local builder set to work. Windows were knocked into the barn that conveniently faced north. Old-fashioned boilers were installed, since, as we lacked electricity, powered fans could not be used. Water was pumped up from a well with an old, electric pump served by an ancient generator which, when it did not break down, provided lighting for the house though power was beyond its means. At bedtime it would be switched off from an outhouse, alive with mice. And if the baby cried at night, I was obliged to use a torch. Had mankind not lived like this since the Stone Age, and come through to spread across the earth and thrive, I pondered when my courage failed.

That winter was the coldest for over half a century. The earth was concrete underfoot and there were days when ice and snow would not permit a motorcar to make it up the steep and stubborn hill. But I was not prepared to wait for the comfortable spring. And hardly were the snowdrops out than we let our London studio house and moved into the frozen wastes of an unfamiliar world where we did not know a soul. Within something like a week, J was happily at work in his splendid studio, from the first light to the last, while with a baby and a six-year-old, a generator and a rattling pump, a boiler fed on solid fuel that it devoured by the ton, and thirteen unfamiliar rooms wrapped in some Chekhovian dream, I had time to take stock and ample opportunity for my favourite pastime of keeping panic well at bay and denying all the fears and terrors in my shaky heart.

Because the scheme was my idea failure was unthinkable, since retracking spelt defeat in my schizoid book of words. Besides, J clearly loved the place and D was settling into school in the little market town of Sudbury, four miles away. If I felt friendless and alone and lost without the old routine of two surgeries a day, had I not come out here to write, like my heroine George Sand?

I did not tell a single soul of my terrors that I might not survive this different and lonely life, where the baby, birds and trees were my only company through endless stretches of the day and night, the shuddering dusk and faltering dawn. I did not even tell myself, except that spring would surely come and summer follow in its wake. And slowly, as the hill turned green and chestnuts held their waxen blooms like candles to the high, curved sky, and swallows occupied their nests, twittering round the tall, grey house, and the baby clapped her hands when a butterfly sailed by, I knew that I must somehow make something of this awesome fate that I had brought upon myself with such heedless recklessness. And as the thistles and the nettles grew and threatened to engulf us all, instead of the roses of my dreams, I determined I would find a gardener who might transform the stubborn clay and unrelenting scene into the landscape of my fantasies.

Lo and behold, the wilderness reverted through the ambling years, back to human ownership. The tangled orchards were restored to fruit. Weeds were scythed from their domain which was slowly laid to lawn. Herbaceous borders reclaimed the soil from nettle, ground elder and thorn. Vegetables stood in rows and chickens followed, in due course, while many different roses bloomed and clambered up the grey brick walls to mellow their austerity. Slowly, with my mother's stubbornness, I rebuilt my Bavarian childhood home for these children of my own, beneath East Anglian skies with their grey and silver domes like a herring trawler's decks. It was no small accomplishment.

Though J protested step by step that the place was good the way it stood, he took real pleasure in the change and even a little pride in walking his acres now so transformed. But underneath smooth surfaces, heartache was slowly building up. If London closes a blind eye to assorted ancestry, the minute Essex is traversed Suffolk with its plaster, lath and thatch propagates conformity. Simple cosmopolitans, we had blundered through these screens of 'Green Man' beer and sugar beet and built our life on feudal land. The hill on which our rectory stood was elevated, it appeared, in senses beyond the geographical. Our Labour poster on the barn that flanked the little, winding lane, ostracized us instantly when the first election came.

In the beginning, when we first moved in, and barn was visibly transformed into a studio, well-intentioned envoys called on these 'settlers' from beyond, drawn by curiosity and traditional courtesy.

'Oh yes, a painter. But *how* nice.' Vivian painted. So did Joan. How *fascinating*, yes, of course. Did J paint lovely horses too, like dear Sir Alfred Munnings did, at Dedham, fifteen miles away, or would he favour dogs or cats, still-life or flowers, possibly?

What they saw pained them, visibly. We should have been prepared for it, and J, by long experience, was. Only I was hurt and crushed by being swiftly written off along with the other 'Londoners' from the new 'overspill estates', the black sheep of the sixties, as far as East Anglia was concerned. What had I done and what was wrong? Unsteady being that I was, my self-image dependent on whatever feedbacks came my way, I took this snubbing personally and felt demolished, written off, less than a beetle or a worm. In my bafflement and rage I grew more arrogant than they. Let them keep their coffee mornings, their home-made jam and flower shows, their produce contests and bazaars – I was now a novelist and had no time for all that, while an infant part of me would have given anything to be asked in from the cold. I took some locum jobs now and then, to make some impact and to show these country bumpkins what was what, but it failed to cut the ice, which had frozen solid from the moment J insisted that no hunt intent on any creature's death should cross a single blade of grass if it grew on our land.

I was wholly at a loss. In leaving London I had left behind my magical persona as instant healer, whereas J had forfeited the magnetism that so readily accrues to artists in the capital.

It suited J extremely well to find his diary a blank. As far as he was concerned this was the object of the exercise. He drew upon his inner world, endlessly, as it appeared, delighting to be left alone to shape his vision here in solitude. But thrown entirely on myself in this unaccustomed way, the abject, new reality left me floundering and aghast. The ostracism shot me down into a pit of hopelessness that I had never bargained for in the easy, urban scene. But I was not defeated yet and raised my battered head to see if there was a remedy.

Since pictures painted must be sold, even by a staunch recluse, the answer presently appeared on my horizons of despair. J's admirers had by now begun to get onto his track. The initial trickle grew into the old, steady stream of the London studio days.

Intellectuals, Yiddishists, patrons, who admired J and flocked to see him and his work, converged upon our rectory, from all the corners of the earth, especially in summer time. These international brigades we labelled 'London Visitors', and we soon came to rely exclusively on them for human contacts of most kinds. All my hungry hopes were pinned on these unsuspecting guests, that they would restore my self-esteem to its earlier minimum, which had allowed me to survive somehow in the tricky world. These hopes, however, proved short-lived. For my inner loneliness only spread and multiplied once I realized their sole aim and object was to visit the studio and its maestro. No one took an interest in the children and myself to match the flow of eulogies that they lavished upon *him*. How was that to be resolved? How was I to find a place in this misdirected sun?

If you cannot beat them, join them, muttered my bewildered mind. If I was of no interest in my own little right, then I would have to come to heel and learn to play the 'artist's wife', straight out of art history. There was, I soon recognized, no shortage of good models there, from Saskia to Cordelia John, with her long red velvet gowns and enticing gypsy smile. I hurled myself into this part with the despairing energy of an inner bankruptcy that must, at all costs, be denied. I would work wonders and generate such a charisma of my own that the world would be agog and J slide slowly out of view before my dazzling radiance. Upon the quagmire of such shifting sands, single-handed, through the years, I conjured such a model of triumphant grandiosity as knew few local parallels. Its raw materials were my scorn and spite, behind which cowered well disguised a ravening appetite for love.

By natural talent an astounding cook, the image I concocted was a unique hotchpotch fantasia. Partly selected from my own parental splendours in Berlin, steeped in the heyday of the bourgeois age, I sprinkled it with earthy spice selected from J's tales of his Warsaw Ghetto days, when, poor and makeshift, it conversed with prophets in its golden age. Attired in picturesque array, I slaved for hours at my fantasy, with quite spectacular results. And yet, the magic did not take.

Those who are hottest on the 'genius trail', often people who project their own creativity into some artist of renown, are by the same invidious laws often obliged to denigrate the 'great one's' close associates with cruel subtlety.

'My, those delicious brussel sprouts . . . you must give me the recipe,' a gilt-edged smile would throw at me, before addressing worthier themes to the maestro's distant end of the old refectory table, long enough to serve a court, that I had located and installed as part of the fine scenery. It could have just as easily been sawn in two, as far as most mealtime conversations went.

Bedevilled months stretched into years. I felt relegated to absolute obscurity and grew increasingly depressed. Like a piece of sewing that had little chance of getting done, I picked up medicine now and then. For a while I even had a little practice of my own. But nothing really seemed to help. Sometimes, of an evening, when the children were in bed, I drove into the market town to visit our GP, and speak of London and the hopes that I had buried, seemingly for good, while I declined the tranquillizers that a new and giddy age proffered from its rainbow shelf. Besides, what hope was there for change which I still imagined lay in the outer, not the inner world. How could the former be exchanged? The children loved the countryside and had their own routine and friends. J appeared happy and content, at least for some more months to come, until that lid was taken off. He was fruitfully at work in his enormous studio set among the rolling fields and elms of Suffolk on the hill above the valley of the Stour.

So the seasons came and went. Great combine harvesters rode their seas. The leaves flowed down, the land was ploughed, the stubble burnt and Christmas came; then snowdrops, like a fleece of hope, lambs and the swallows back again. An ancient chestnut in our grounds served as the disbanding post of flocks from all the neighbourhood. Wild with excitement that they had survived the perils of their epic flight to recognize old nesting sites and well-known landmarks once again, their effervescence filled the skies. On such May evenings I would mourn: if only, only, little birds, I could also feel like you and grow to love this stubborn land that turns its back on me and mine. But there was even worse to come.

One autumn day, at a morning hour when otherwise he would have been working, J came to me in great despair. He said he could no longer paint and lived in panic and continuous fear as of some impending doom or absolute catastrophe. Our kindly doctor muttered this or that, akin to some old country spells, and naturally gave him pills. Predictably nothing changed. I took the law into my poor, mad hands in search of instant panaceas, and took us all to Mexico; time-honoured cure by change of scene: faith in the efficacy of Spas.

We landed on this Southern moon and took a house in central Mexico. An ancient culture peered at us through dark, uncomprehending eyes. At night the dogs howled in an Indian tongue. At an altitude of some twelve thousand feet, I hallucinated in the icy mountain night. I heard the earth quake raucously as a forewarning of the end, but thought a virus was to blame. Looking back on it today, I have no doubt that madness had all but struck, so dangerously far from home, with two small children in our care.

J rallied somewhat at my plight. I lay in bed. The doctor came. He sent his nuns, by taxi, twice a day. They spoke a rapid, Spanish prayer and gave me penicillin shots. Men brought us wood, so we had fires. A silent woman swept the place. We kept the fires going at night to keep the cold and dark at bay. Mornings, the sun was back again. Wrapped in blankets, Indians stood to soak its warmth up with their bones.

This modicum of mothering put me on my feet again. We haunted Mexico a while, valley to valley, coast to coast, a little family of four, wholly makeshift, wholly lost, inconsequential in this Aztec land, and then flew back to whence we came, too sick and shaken for a word of hope; too blank to seek true remedy.

That was in February. By May the alarming abcess had burst. Our little S, then almost four, found some 'major tranquillizers' that were in my doctor's bag. They shone like smarties in her eyes. When she stopped breathing the first night in the local hospital, sitting vigil at her side, I was the first to notice it, and nothing seemed to be to hand to meet this grave emergency. When the trolley came at last tubes for intubation were not of the appropriate size and I was hustled from the scene. Probably already dead, she lay in 'full intensive care' and 'died' upon the seventh day.

At the funeral, J and I sat side by side entirely alone. Entirely alone we stood and saw the little coffin slide through the dim, eternal doors, then drove home without a word. Within several weeks I lost the baby I was carrying. I nearly died from loss of blood because I felt too bad to care.

When I was on my feet once more, full of someone else's blood, and barely able to take note of what was really happening, the awful truth had to be faced that J was almost beyond help. He lay unshaven and unwashed, mute and helpless, past repair, stiff with suicidal thoughts, convinced that he would act them out. I gave my village practice up to become a full-time nurse, and hid all razors, knives, blades, tablets and ropes and deadly things. I hoped that simple, loving care would put him on his feet again. But J drowsed heavy and inert, with unrecognizing eyes, through the shortening autumn days. Christmas only made him worse.

I gathered every ounce of strength and drove him up to London where they took him into hospital. It meant we had to be apart, since I felt that school routine was everything poor D still had, but I was simply paranoid about East Anglian hospitals. Never again, I reasoned in those frightful days, would I entrust someone I loved to any nurse or doctor there. But so malignant was the case that the broken heart did not respond to any answer on the daunting list of physical psychiatry.

I commuted to and fro and struggled to maintain for D some semblance of normality. 'The London Visitors', of course, had vanished at the sight of death, the hint of fresh catastrophe. I could not even seem to raise a rota to visit J on days I had to stay at home. It seemed we three were all alone, in a forsaken unfamiliar world.

When, with the approach of spring, we had almost given up hope that anything would work for J, a substance called Trimipramine had just been marketed in France. It was the sixth month of a living death when J sat up and smiled again. To this day I do not believe that it was in fact the drug, but that this was a symbol for refusal to abandon hope on the part of all concerned who manned and held that dismal scene.

In due course J was back at home, first for weekends, then for good, on a fearsome list of drugs, pink and white and green and blue. We had won a breathing space. Tablets were sustaining J, while my own battle between life and death was only starting to be joined. But the thrust of life was strong, despite the serious handicaps. After losing three small girls, I longed to bring a daughter up. And after many daunting trials, we finally adopted B, a West Indian baby girl. We sold the great, grey rectory that stood for so much tragedy, and bought a village former school, whose schoolrooms made a studio.

While this move had still left D with access to his old school, it had brought Cambridge within reach of a straight cross-country drive. So in this modest breathing space, I took the opportunity to see a Cambridge psychoanalyst regarding my own state of mind after all these grim events. He listened to me carefully, then said that he was as depressed and had, in fact, no vacancy. And so I drove back home again, still uncertain and perplexed, but not sufficiently composed to take the matter further, then. In any case, was there a need?

J was working once again. To my envy and relief the studio of our village house was humming as in happier days. D and B were doing well. As mothers all too often do, I was inclined to see myself as an extension of my family, dissolving my own needs in theirs. Counting the blessings that I had, I let the question of more treatment slide, first, into sheer *laissez-faire*, and then be torn out of my hands by a newly gathering storm.

My father, who was ninety then, and lived in Hamburg, all alone, phoned to say that he was ill and coming for the Christmas days. We had not met for some ten years. I drove to Harwich, through the icy dark, to meet the ferry in the night. As there was nobody around, the port officials let me bring the car alongside, just for once. Down the floodlit gangway groped a broken, clearly dying man. Grey, in the cruel neon lights, still immaculately dressed, one hand clutched the gangway rail, the other, presents he had brought, just as in the olden days, returning from some business trip to The Family in Berlin.

Man of the world that he had been, a connoisseur and gourmet once known to put the fear of God into the most dazzling chefs, wine-waiters and their ranks-in-arms, he now sat slippered by the fire enjoying a small dish of porridge, full of praise for everyone and everything we did for him. Each morning when I made his bed it was as though a ghost had lain, so undisturbed the bed remained, as though this gentle visitor, so unlike his former self, was no longer of this wintry world.

Within a week of getting back, for he would hear of nothing else, he took an overdose, as planned. In his room in the hotel where he had lived in recent years, they found him sitting in a chair, in bow-tie and a fine, black suit, as though about to take the lift to the foyer and the dining hall, passport and bank-book on his lap, in a deep and final sleep.

His whole life's savings had been used up by the German doctors' bills. Cancer was eating at his bones, and he had decided it was time to leave the little that remained to the local medical school. And for each grandchild he had set aside something like four hundred pounds.

For seven days and nights he lay, just like little S had done, unconscious in a hospital. The old, old vigil once again, sitting cold and stiff with fear by a silent telephone: this time, that he might survive when his wish was otherwise. Calls to Hamburg, every night, praying that he might die in peace and somehow manage to escape modern medicine's idiocy. But when he had eluded them, nevertheless, his death proved more than my last residues of strength could take.

My breakdown took a tragic course. I blamed poor J for everything, insisting we must separate. At this point someone should have screamed that I was mad and that he was mad if he complied with such a wish. But no one said it. No one spoke those urgent and essential words. As rats will leave a sinking ship, we were abandoned by the world. The last thing I remember was a package that my mother sent. There was a necklace and a brooch, and underneath a little note. It said her woman friend had died the same day that my father had, so she no longer had a wish to remain alive herself.

She had suffered a nervous breakdown some twelve years or so before. Although much stronger, after that, I knew that she would always lapse into precarious states and that I needed her alive desperately at this time. If my mother also died, how could I myself survive such a sudden holocaust? In a blind and frenzied state I telephoned her GP who hurried round immediately and arrived there just in time to keep vigil with her grief. After that my world went dark, like an extinguished shooting star.

At my own mad wish I stayed behind in Suffolk, broken and alone, with two children in my care. At this point the village took to persecuting little B, seeing that the child was 'black'. In the mornings 'Nig-Nog Street' was scrawled in mud on our white gates. Wild with fury, I lashed back through the pages of the local press. The national press took up the tale, earning me some further hate. In between I lay in bed, as J had done in earlier days, while the children were at school. When they were home I dragged myself around the kitchen and the house like a wounded animal. J came at weekends, every week. And every Sunday he would go and I could not say the words: how much, how much we needed him. And when I could, he could not hear, hurt and weary, past belief. Neither of us realized then how enduring was our love, given a modicum of help. But I was not quite beaten yet. Some part of me kept holding on, for dear life and for all of us. One day, I dragged myself at last to London – back to V for help. My Jungian Mother offered me an appointment the same day.

'Get back into analysis,' she urged me, almost instantly.

Her words came as a huge relief. Regardless of what the other had said in Cambridge recently, help was permitted me, it seemed. I had a right to ask for help after all, another time.

Sitting in her room again, in a quite bedraggled state, my eyes inflamed from constant tears, I slowly focused, with her words, on a foundation we had laid together in those distant years, whatever else we had not done. As I drank her cup of tea, this reassurance helped me to pick my scattered fragments up and tack them into something like the experience of a whole. Gradually it dawned on me that I was not beyond the pale, as I had recently assumed. That same evening I was back in the village solitude, a prisoner of the old routine. But now I saw a gleam of hope: was Cambridge not within my reach?

Therapeutic Interlude

I would have given almost anything for the opportunity to return to London there and then to start my new analysis. But D's 'O' levels were by now just another year away, preventing any change of school until that hurdle had been cleared. Surely Cambridge had to have more resources than the one gloomy psychoanalyst who had discouraged me so much when I had consulted him?

Yes, a friend of mine replied, a retired therapist lived on the edges of the town and still took patients now and then, the more so if they were short-term.

Two charming whippets peered at me through a landing window when I arrived and rang the bell. The door was opened by a frail, bent man. The hand he gave me so readily felt like the warm nest of a tired bird and seemed to crumple in my own, yet the blue, seafaring eyes chased the weariness away as though one had imagined it. His much-adapted, well-worn house, was a comforting affair set in gardens that an old, gnarled man – the archetypal gardener – tended in the timeless way habitual to monasteries; his barrows, rakes and twiglike brooms appearing dreamlike here or there.

I had been told that CS was a poet of undoubted gifts. An erudite and gentle man, more scholar than mere scientist, I warmed to him spontaneously, and when we reached his first-floor room, burst into floods of tears at once: 'I have done nothing except cook my life away for ten whole years, and write a novel no one wants, while my husband's pictures are in continuous demand. Everyone wants only J, and no one finds me interesting and that is never going to change.'

I sat and wept for half an hour, while he waited quietly, clearly accustomed to such overtures.

'But you are here now,' he replied with a courteous little smile.

Eclectic in a home-brewed sweep, he was basically a Freudian, and gradually instilled in me a taste for that great edifice I had been skirting to my cost. I would not presume to judge just how competent he was by the later standards I acquired, based upon concepts of their own, for this remarkable old man was largely outside categories, thanks to the accomplishment of an integral and well-seated soul, as is all too rarely found in the orthodox professional ranks.

I went to see him twice a week, lay on his simple, generous couch, felt contained by his staunch support and started thinking that perhaps I had a future once again, instead of nothing but a broken past. As the project gathered shape it spelt out London, where I could begin a new analysis. Then, step by step, the wish emerged to take a training course, to become a psychotherapist myself, even if I was forty-six.

Such new-found aspirations meant that I had somehow now to rise above the bevy of my fears and put this year to fullest use. However dithery I felt, however shaky and afraid of stepping back into the world, where skills were learnt and new professions forged, I had, I realized, to emerge from this village-purdah now and pull all sorts of different strings that happened to be dangling within reach the minute I looked for them. And CS, knowing that we had little longer than a year, focused very sensibly on the misgivings and fears that now bedevilled every move to shoulder my own life again, once the habit had been lost.

As my shaky confidence was very gradually restored by the psychotherapy, the 'Married Women Doctors' scheme that had been recently evolved came to my rescue generously. Designed for those who, like myself, had grown rusty at the kitchen sink and wished to enter a new speciality, it supplied appropriate work in allocated hospitals on a part-time basis first, to facilitate a smooth return. The pay was modest, but extremely fair, based on previous salary, status and experience. The thought of *any* salary struck me as a miracle in my self-devalued state where I felt such a heap of rags.

Fulbourne Mental Hospital, serving Cambridge and her shires, and only twenty miles away, offered me this sort of job. An ancient, sprawling edifice, it had been pulled and pushed and tugged into the twentieth century, only fairly recently, to be an 'open' hospital. Gone were the locks and jangling keys and horrors of my student days, which had really scared me out of specializing in psychiatry when I was newly qualified. A kindly atmosphere prevailed. Since the place now saw itself as a 'psychotherapeutic community', decisions could be shared by all the various members of staff, regardless of seniority. Despite life's usual ups and downs, the scene was a supportive one, aiming at democracy, and scrutinizing where this failed with steadfastness and honesty.

I was allocated to a progressive long-stay ward, struggling to rehabilitate patients quite determined to end their days tucked up inside, even though some of them were young. Since I had grave uncertainties on that very score myself: did I want to make a move or regress entirely, I was at times quite confused as to the dividing line between the patients and myself. This predicament is not uncommon with psychiatrists, in my own experience. Considering such handicaps things went reasonably well. And if I didn't have a clue, that was what the job was for, I kept comforting myself, with assistance from CS on two afternoons each week. If everything kept going round in a most unnatural way, an actual epidemic came to the rescue graciously. Numbers of the staff went down with what was very neatly called 'labyrinthitis' of the inner ear, where the sense of balance lies.

Certainly medicine has this knack of christening, with a high-flown name, each aberration of the human soul, thereby relieving the psychiatrist of untold case material. On some days I could hardly drive; on others hardly sit or stand or walk. But naturally, there was a pill, and others had the syndrome too, who also walked the hospital like sailors walk a rolling deck; and in that way a serious 'conversion' symptom was ignored. Besides, I had 'no time for that', having embarked on a career to show that I was after all someone to be reckoned with, and every bit as good as J.

But, in my precarious state, there were lapses now and then, and matters came to a head in which the Bishop and myself got into an awesome fray. A clergyman, his wife and son were admitted to my ward, jointly, as a family, although the boy was soon discharged. The circumstances were, in fact, quite exceptionally sad. The wife and husband had been found, frozen, starved, in matted rags, in some sort of makeshift house in a village in the Fens. The madness they colluded in is known as a *Folie à deux*. The wife felt terrified of 'germs', wherefore neither food, nor clothes, nor bedding, neither child nor mate, could conceivably be touched; and both had acted these delusions out in a controlled and obsessional way, screaming quite obscene abuse at all hours of the night and lapsing into silence in the day. All their money had been spent on disinfectants that were found by the gallon in the empty house. Both were emaciated to a bone, covered in ulcers, wounds and scabs. And all this had been going on in a village, month by month, while folk pretended ignorance, despite all the gossip flying round. Only when the wretched man ran stark naked through the streets, exhibiting his Job-like state, had someone called an ambulance in the interests of propriety. And now, the remedy was up to me. Or so, at any rate, I thought, brimming with omnipotence.

I took a careful history. Vicar, wife and children had inhabited a rectory, where the demented couple had a 'living' of a modest sort in a parish not too far from the one where they were found. After several reasonable years, they drew the curtains on themselves, and were no longer seen in church. Christenings and funerals soon fell into sad arrears, and, in response to agonized complaints, other vicars had to come and set some kind of rota up. If senior members of the Church called to sort the trouble out the doors were bolted, entrance was barred. Crested letters were returned. Horrid language could be heard reverberating through the quiet air. At last some higher council met to vote the man be pensioned off. Indeed, what else was there to do? He had been briefly hospitalized in a local hospital. There, I saw from the reports, he had been treated by the dermatologist for the ulcers on his legs, and next, by the physician for malnutrition of an unknown, stubborn kind.

While he was in this hospital the rambling rectory burnt down. No one knew just how or why. His wife and children nearly lost their lives. Not a stone or brick remained. Not a rag or beam or bean. Mercifully the building was adequately insured but their belongings were not. Everything they owned was lost: 'living', furniture, the lot. The Church then bought them a small house that no one had seen fit to modernize. Damp and cold, with bare earth floors and condensation running down the walls, it was their stable at the time these survivors fell into my care. I still remember the waves of shock that swept through the hospital, a place accustomed to man's frailty. It was as though we had stumbled on Hell's outposts in our very midst, in slumbering East Anglia.

In my soul the case touched off a towering rage and terrible despair. In this hapless family I recognized something similar to our recent plight in these very godless shires, for all its thanksgiving and hymns. And way beyond, my blazing eyes stared down the terrible decades to the gas- and smoke-filled corridors of the extermination camps. In that precarious state of mind, I had the social worker write to the august powers that be, in that ancient house of God that soared above the brackish Fens, that it was up to them to make provision for this man who had devoted all his life to the service of the Church. Back came an erudite reply, which wholly failed to meet the bill, together with gifts of nightwear: charity.

At that point something in me blew. Unpractised in diplomacy, I snatched the law into my trembling hands and, upon hospital stationery, wrote to, or rather thundered at, the Bishop, no one lesser, that Christ be damned, the time had come to be a little human, yes! I had stirred up a hornet's nest. The Bishop was, it transpired, a VIP on the Hospital Board: an awesome concoction of gowns and flowered hats and ancient, whited sepulchres who, as befits good noblemen, rallied to the defenceless mad against outrageous people like myself. Further, there were certain funds that he was empowered to withhold. Such was the consternation that I really felt he was able to deflect God's love and blessing from us all and relegate the entire establishment to Hell for all eternity. These were the fantasies, I fear, that his displeasure had unleashed among these good psychiatrists; and it was all, entirely, my fault. If I did not write at once, and offer my apologies, and take back everything I'd said . . .

I sat and sat and thought it through in a state of hate and rage that matched the Bishop's, at a guess. Christ stood staunchly at my side, in those endless dialogues. Christ was right and I was right, and the Bishop could go to Hell. But what on earth was I to do? They'd told me, fair and square, that if I disobeyed them now, I would lose my job. This as a budding pragmatist I could not contemplate. It was my bridgehead to the world.

After several sleepless nights, I reached a sneaky compromise. I wrote that I owed him an apology for having said the things I said on official stationery, and for speaking on my colleagues' behalf when I had not consulted them. Back, on crested paper, came complete forgiveness by return of post and happy wishes for fair Christmas-tide. After the holidays I heard that my vicar's pension had been raised, doubled, if I recall aright, and help had come in from all sides offering to modernize the shack, to visit them on their return and make amends for all the past: social psychiatry from God above.

Meanwhile, my thoughts turned more and more to London: a new start in life and training possibilities, even if I was terrified at the thought of interviews that I did not expect to pass. Yet I somehow managed to pull the wool over their eyes and to my amazement and relief I was accepted for the course. So, I had not been written off. That wider world still wanted me, was offering me another chance. I chewed my fingers in delight and fear. Which was the greater it would be hard to say.

So much for the light of day.

At night I had disturbing dreams of huge, wild seas that broke over my head, tossing splintered furniture. Waves rose like monsters from the deep, carrying in their frothy arms the holds of foundered vessels, riven ships, remains of sailors in their ghostly shrouds.

'They sound like schizophrenic dreams,' my kindly therapist would muse. But here, he was out of his depth. He did not know the deeper fears that my new energies would now put to wild, destructive use.

Sometimes my bed went spinning round, like some grotesque invention at a fair, and I would have to hold on with both hands, if I was not to be flung out over the head of pin-point crowds, strewn like black ashes on the ground below, while droves of tadpoles swam around. By day these apparitions would vanish as though stowed away in secret lockers, trapdoors in the floor. The decks would dry and calm return. The daylight hours were my reprieve: work, children, psychotherapy, and plans and hopes Everest-high.

One more hurdle lay ahead: to find a suitable school for D.

'It is unusual,' wrote the famous school, 'to take a boy into "the sixth".'

'Alright,' they ceded. 'Interviews for special applicants in spring.'

If I insisted, very well; they would see us in the autumn: now. The other side had been subdued by a barrage from my guns.

A being in top hat, gloves and tails, straight out of *David Copperfield*, ushered us both into a tiny room. Some heartbeats later he was back.

'Will the boy please follow me.'

Moving no single muscle in his wax-cast face, he spoke in the lugubrious tones that legendary henchmen use. I shivered, feeling I might not ever see my son again. And yet, I knew, I had to win this stark, Wagnerian ordeal.

'Now Madam, you will follow me.'

Behold, the messenger was back, albeit without my child who was the apple of my eye. I followed him up solemn stairs. The Highmaster awaited me.

'Madam,' said he, in the same voice – was it the same man, but disguised? – 'You and I are now about to take a turn about the grounds.'

Braving an awesome autumn gale, sweeping the leaves before it, and a hint of rain, and marching at such a fearful pace that I despaired of keeping up in my unaccustomed, fancy shoes, I was addressed at wind-torn intervals.

'Madam, I have to tell you first of all, your typewriter spelt so horribly, I must confess I had not planned to take this application up. However, it would now appear, the boy knows an astonishing amount. Really astonishing, indeed. Of course, you've got to understand, he's been a big fish in a little pond.'

With this he stopped and swung around, glowering at me through the season's squalls, sizing me up from head to foot, as though to ascertain the breeding stock of a somewhat baffling mare, whose stable was alarmingly obscure. The whole ordeal was obviously attuned to dukes and dowagers, I mourned, feeling defeated, when he snapped: 'So, Madam, he has got a place. Whatever further questions you may have, you will address them to my deputy. He will be sending you the usual forms.'

All at once I found myself back to normality once more: the sounds and flavours of the daily world, and D beside me, as before. Our rural life was coming to a close. The village house went up for sale. By early summer it was sold. A little cottage had been bought, almost adjoining D's new school so as to save commuting time during the 'A' level years. Just across the road we found a quiet kindly school for B that seemed entirely right for her. Neither was our little world more than a mile or so from J, installed in the old studio house which we had hung on to through the years.

So, hour by hour and day by day, London assumed reality. Then summer finally crossed the calendar past D's 'O' levels. I counted those last, endless days like a prisoner in a cell, waiting, waiting for release. How those East Anglian June days dragged in that village which I loathed, where I was on speaking terms with hardly a living soul, with projections, blind as bats, circling in the evening air.

Even the parting from CS I skimmed through in the facile way that is habitual to the splintered mind which knows no way of making roots for fear of having them torn up. My Fulbourne patients, equally, watched my going sullenly, while some hid in a bed or chair or threw their dinner on the floor. None of us was able to look at separation pains or handle the resulting fears and deeply threatening fantasies.

At last, the final hour came. The removal van had pulled away heading for London, finally, with all our worldly goods inside. I turned the key upon the old oak door and left it with the shop next door where they received it silently. About to leap into the car, I realized that the cat had gone. A last mad search for our staunch tom, with his frayed and battered ears. The cat was nowhere to be seen. He had decided he would stay among his kith and progeny. B's tears were flowing for her cat, her school, her friends, her whole life: all going to be left behind. D shared her feelings, numb with rage that for the first time in his life I was putting myself first. Irritated by their grief that threatened my euphoria, I now felt angry and alone, and offered little sympathy. I turned the hard ignition key, put the estate car into gear, and felt it like a ferry boat, pulling slowly on mysterious oars, across the old black river Styx into my light of day once more.

My Freudian Father

The heat lay heavy on the land in that July of 1973. The trees drowsed dusty, somnolent and still. The air was syrupy by day and like a tepid bath at night. Suffolk, Essex, Hertfordshire, were briefly nudged by our tyres and then curled over once again to dream their stubborn history, on which we no more scratched our mark than hens on farmyard dust. Each wrapped in sorrows of their own, both D and B had fallen fast asleep, by way of simple, human self-defence, long before London straggled into sight. And so I greeted her alone, my beloved megalith.

How I had missed her, through those Suffolk years. Past rhyme and reason I had yearned for my old mother of the Blitz. How often she had held my hand when there had been nobody else. There, all my children had been born. My small and her majestic span had brushed so often in the dusk and dawn. And now they touched another time, for some still hidden, and unwritten page.

Such were the sentiments with which I made that hot, homesick drive, to start up up my shrill, persistent, organ-grinder life at some new and hopeful pitch. As is frequently the case when one pins unrealistic hopes upon a change of outer scene, the city of my dreams now seemed less than a total panacea.

The yearly ritual of the summer holiday had swept most former friends away to enjoy the very tranquillity that I had spurned so blantantly and was half longing to retrieve, as a shelter from new cares. After the ready access to green fields, wide, sweeping vistas of the countryside and generous spaciousness of country homes, it seemed a cramped and box-like little house that I had managed to secure as the headquarters for our brand new life. B, with her love of running wild and animals of every kind, felt intolerably cooped up. Nor did she have a single friend. I did not know it, at the time, but both the children and myself grew increasingly depressed and deeply hopeless, day by day. Trapped in the broiling concrete wastes, with no distraction or relief and no friends to hand, the break-up of our family that I had wilfully provoked began to strike home forcibly with a grim finality that I myself frenetically denied, absolutely terrified to question any of my acts for fear of finding a mistake; since my judgement had to be flawless in my perfect eyes.

J suffered uncomplainingly. Accustomed to the blows of fate, he bore his sorrows stoically. The children sulked, lost their appetite, watched television endlessly in the airless little house, two apathetic caricatures of their former, vigorous selves. Completely out of touch with our abject state of loss, I brashly pursued my bright 'new life', treading in the well-worn steps of several of my women friends who were self-styled feminists. In growing numbers they had run like lemmings to the early death of marriages that might have been rendered seaworthy again, shuttling children here and there, sometimes to their long-term doom, in answer to the clarion call of misguided activists who recanted later on, often when it was too late. But at the time my batty fantasies enjoyed free rein to idealize the 'endless possibilities' that would later peter out into lonely, single lives plagued by self-doubt and remorse.

J would visit frequently. At other times, we all went out, a make-believe small family, locked into four apathies, unable to communicate and hammer out some remedy, or at the very least to share our endless, private miseries. Yet that was hardly possible when I continuously denied how much we were all suffering, and J did not feel qualified to bring influence to bear, terrified that I might break down completely if he interfered with my state of mind, fragile as it was. Besides, my bandwagon had gained such wild momentum by this time: a life that was my very own and whose pace nothing could slow down.

Had someone taken me to task and told me that I ought to wait, at least until the autumn term offered the children a routine, I would have almost certainly had hysterics on the spot. For I had no inkling yet that a truly separate life has never been required to serve as an altar for human sacrifice. Blind with terror that the prize would be wrested from me at this hour when my 'final chance' had come, I snatched at any instant work, simply that I might be seen to be standing on my own two feet, however much my legs might shake.

In the summer season, when GPs want locums urgently, a living was not hard to find. Smothering panic, I soon picked up those well-worn threads again, given a quick refresher course in the latest pharmacology by smooth-tongued drug company salesmen who hovered in the waiting room at the end of morning surgery, their lessons always reinforced with pathetic little bribes: diaries, calendars and pens in which doctors take delight.

I installed a young au pair. Polish, Wanda could hardly speak three words of English at the time. Consequently B was left, a bewildered six-year-old, friendless, with a foreign girl who could only smile at her, while her mother came and went like a galleon whose sails were filled with self-importance; D took refuge in his books, fearful of the autumn term in an unfamiliar school where, instead of intimates, strangers were awaiting him. But where my children were concerned, I was clearly deaf and blind.

For me, September arrived like the answer to a prayer. I found a psychiatric job in a mental hospital, and my training course began with its evening seminars: the basic ABC of Freud. Life had started at long last.

With an interesting job and the training course transformed from dream into reality, I now readily mislaid the object of the exercise: proper treatment for myself, since old defences of denial had snatched the reins once again. The course left me entirely free to choose a Freudian analyst, as long as he was 'recognized' for their training purposes. Some part of me must have known how crucial this decision was. But, in my self-defeating way, I had conveniently 'forgotten' just how ill I had been only a few months ago. 'That was Suffolk,' I believed. That was all 'past history'. If the course required that I have some psychotherapy as part of its requirements, I would leave that choice to them. Very likely 'they knew best', my usual confusions ran.

I was still unable to take responsibility for an issue that was now central to my shaky life. I had recognized this truth well enough a year before in my rural solitude with its threatened states of mind but had laid these matters well aside in the old, habitual way of those who dream their life away, hardly knowing where it goes because they are afraid to wrest the tiller into their own hands.

99

'Their choice' for me, accordingly, fell through my letter box one day of silvery October mists.

Always readily seduced by outermost appearances, I was instantly entranced by the Freudian therapist to whom they had allocated me. The spitting image of an ageing Highland laird, his courteous manner and warming smile drew me to him instantly. His ambience of the 'wise old man' linked him to my Jungian days, on this unknown Freudian path. There was a wealth of flowering plants on every inch of windowsill, and tantalizing kitchen smells perfumed the lofty entrance hall. Hardly was I through the door before I loved this cosy house, where generations shared a life of music, laughter, books and toys, an unbroken stream of memories.

If my own marriage, at the time, was severed and ripped apart, this solid, grandparental home instilled in me a growing trust that family life can run its course from birth to death, encompassing not just one or two but three generations in its stride. And it was here, in Dr B's home, that this idea took hold of me like the answer to some prayer. So many of my then friends had kept stale marriages on ice until 'the children started school', or 'went to secondary school', or 'were old enough to understand' or could 'manage for themselves' that I had never paused to think what these fractured images might mean in deeper human terms.

It was the ambience of this gracious family home that eventually proved to be the enduring benefit of this Freudian therapy. Not the analytic work, but this example now persuaded me that J, the children and myself should live under one roof again. And this we managed to achieve two years later, by which time the psychotherapy itself had floundered irretrievably. Why should this have been the case?

RB had simply no idea that he had been entrusted with the pieces of a splintered child. She had come to him disguised as a mother, wife and doctor dressed up with a confident panache, while many Freudian workshops, in my own experience, lack the appropriate instruments to pierce this preposterous defence. That behind this brash façade, a very frightened urchin crouched, who bit and hissed and screeched and spat at anyone who came too close, like a starving small stray cat abandoned in an empty house, never dawned on poor RB. But then my interviewers for the

Course had similarly been taken in. Where then did the trouble lie?

Freud had only got as far as his own self-analysis, one of the great feats of mankind. Mrs Klein, his follower, who began to analyse little children, was soon to find, however, that the discoveries of Freud had a distinct prehistory, related intimately to the very earliest months of life. And it is on these earliest months that a sound analysis needs to focus from the start.

If one finds an infant crying in a cold, dark street, because his mother has got lost and he fears that he will die, it is no use offering irrelevant distractions. That baby needs to be reunited with his mother, which applied to myself. For the baby part of me was utterly refusing to be sidetracked or fobbed off with yet another therapy that knew nothing of the roots of my wild anxieties but only activated them. Uppermost were my fears that my infantile demands would exhaust my therapist and that he would consequently die. Such a dread is deeply rooted in the early infant mind. When a hungry, empty baby comes to a nice full breast and empties it, as he fills up, he sees the breast and himself as a closed hydraulic system. He does not yet know that the breast can replenish its supplies, and may feel terror-stricken that he has emptied it for good with his greedy appetite. Unaware of this, RB interpreted what I was saying, all of which was pointing to such fears, at a veiled and deeper level, as my wish that he should die out of some hostility founded upon penis envy. So early in the analysis I could not possibly have been near those later conflicts. In developmental terms, if I could even be described as severed from a placenta yet, I was still struggling to possess Mother's body and her breast to the exclusion of all else. Moreover this mother was still experienced in terms of 'parts', long before she would become familiar as a whole. My thinly veiled hostility, my wild anxieties that I was not understood, all this primitive material slowly induced in poor RB a crisis of self-confidence, whose signals I was picking up to multiply my other fears. But looking back on it today, the most disturbing aspect was that RB never used the essential 'transference' with that detailed, close precision that a Kleinian will do, to bring the here and now to life. To analyse the transference in a stable setting is the basic, fundamental task of every analysis. Here is the road that will lead step by step to where the basic problems lie, in each individual case. But, where it is not pursued and investigated day by day, then these feelings overflow into excessive 'acting out'. This is the phenomenon which made the worthy Dr Breuer retire in full haste from the fray when his patient, Anna O, became wildly amorous. Faced with the same incubus, Freud had firmly stood his ground until this latest mystery yielded its dark secrets up. From then on, once the transference was scrupulously analysed, instead of being acted out, all concerned were mercifully spared these humiliating scenes.

Not so in my therapy. Both 'negative' and 'positive' areas of the transference, in other words, both hate and love, lay equally neglected, clamouring for some release regardless of whether the route was appropriate or not. The negative became displaced onto the actual training course, whose obtuse rigidities served to make it a scapegoat. The goat responded and promptly declared me Black Sheep Number One.

But graver trouble was to spring from my loving feelings that cavorted, quite unanalysed. As if a laughing God had tipped an amorous potion in my coffee mug, I now began to 'fall in love' with the most unlikely candidates, like some blithe spirit from a comedy. For winter weeks and summer months I wearied my deaf therapist almost to death with these romantic fantasies which he seemed unable to decode, which would have helped me to express my loving feelings towards him. A love which I felt no one had ever wanted to accept, let alone reciprocate, after my first Nanny left; a love which, seen in baby terms, had been a serious affair. Never again, in later life, would any partner have to wield such precise, responsive skills, if only our first love satisfied the finickety brouhaha and clamour of our earliest needs.

But now, alas, my therapist turned as starchy and remote as my childhood figures had. And, as the summer break approached, fraught with separation fears that got no airing on this Freudian couch, the total hotch-potch drove me to fantasies of entanglements that multipled and ran amok like rabbits on a fertility drug. Consequently I proposed to a consultant whom I liked that we run away together for the coming summer weeks. And it was certainly as well that this kind, goodnatured man was at that time near the end of his Kleinian analysis. Therefore he could gently smile the heated proposition off in lucid and constructive terms that gave me serious food for thought concerning my own therapy and the impasse it had reached, even if the penny failed to drop into its proper slot for some further months to come.

On such confused and dangerous ground, my second year of Freudian psychotherapy presently began. The house I visited three times a week still served as model, and RB seemed as kind and upright as before. So what, I mused, was going wrong? The question was a frightening one, all the more so since I had no conceptual answer yet, while my intuition sensed that we were simply not approaching the layers where my illness lay rumbling in some deep volcano that seemed about to erupt. And no sooner was it posed than I was tempted to deny its implications that I must find another therapist. For this step threatened to disrupt the strenuous struggle to complete my training which was nothing less than the goal of all my dreams. And therefore, in my usual way, I started to prevaricate, until these hard-won inner truths were very nearly swept aside.

Was it, I comforted myself, perhaps a question of more time? What was a year, when all was said and done? Besides, there could be little doubt that areas of valid work had been accomplished, here and there, among the debris of the blistered scene. Somehow, for instance, I had discovered how I kept 'splitting' constantly, which meant that people close to me would for some reason still beyond my grasp, change instantly from black to white, from wholly good to wholly bad, and just as quickly back again. That these wild and sudden swings reflected alternating love and hate in my feelings for RB was sadly never analysed.

As the second training year bumped along this rutted course some inmost oracle began increasingly to prophesy complete disaster if I continued to ignore its warnings to break off this so-called psychotherapy, to go in search of expert help as an absolute priority, even if I was expelled from the unbending training course; especially since my daily work with psychotic patients in the mental hospital was adding greatly to the strain.

But while this impasse persisted and a baffling darkness ruled in my psychotherapy, a faint and very wintry dawn was slowly breaking on the skies of that same workaday scene. Housed in a small bungalow situated in the grounds of a gaunt mental hospital, the unit carried on the task of a psychotherapeutic community. The patients whom we treated there were mainly young adults,

103

and my own work was supervised in seminars and individually by several psychoanalysts whose style, I slowly recognized, was altogether different from RB's blanketed attempt. It had directness and immediacy and brought prompt, clinical relief. Here was an approach that worked: that promised confidence and hope, even with all due regard for the difficulties of the task. Who were these beautiful, white swans? How did they differ from RB, since they too were Freudians? What were these concepts to which my course made no single reference?

The understanding they possessed I was also groping for. Here was the clarity I had equated with analysis from the outset of my quest. Why had it eluded me? Such were the questions racing through my ugly duckling soul. Ashamed of my own ignorance I kept these questions strictly to myself, but lost no opportunity for taking in each single word to apply it to my work, and also to my own, sad case. I found that it seemed to help, this furtive, struggling attempt at hearsay self-analysis. And so the winter months dragged by.

The course had ceased to satisfy my intellectual appetite. Only at the hospital did I continually catch bright and tantalizing glimpses of different concepts, that made sense, only to lose them again in muddled sessions with RB, while I kept avidly alert for any further sign or clue that might lead towards the light.

One day, our unit team was joined by M, a colleague from abroad. A Freudian 'training' analyst in his native Italy, he had given this status up to come to London, he explained. He did not like our weather much nor the food, nor yet his rented flat. Language problems troubled him to an obvious degree. He seemed bemused and somewhat lost. And so I picked my courage up and asked him when we were alone why he was doing all of this? Why had he given up so much? What was he getting in return? I told him I knew Italy, its mountains and coasts, its vitality, and so could readily imagine that he felt homesick now and sad; but would he please enlighten me as to the object of the exercise.

'I've been commuting for a year and it became impossible.'

'For what,' I asked, still more amazed.

'My Kleinian analysis.' He then explained that travelling here twice a week, as he had been doing, was simply not enough; he must live and work here now so that he could go five times a week.

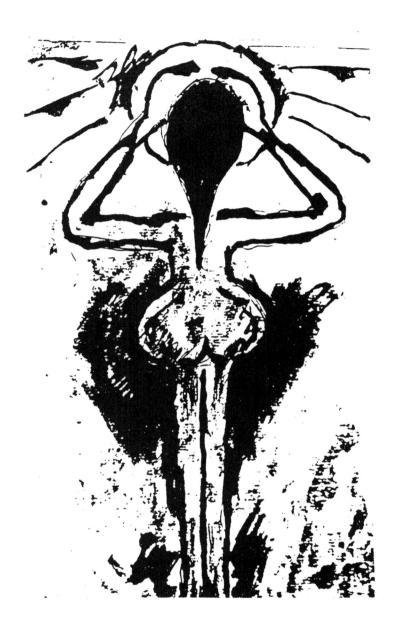

He and his wife had talked it through. He knew there was no other way.

'But why?' I pleaded, 'tell me why. Please tell me, I have got to know.' I sat and listened, horror-struck and fascinated and enthralled by all the implications that these words must surely hold for me.

So they are Kleinians, my swans, I kept repeating to myself, on the daily motorway, ten miles there and ten miles back, that spring of 1975. My age was half a century.

'But *why*?' I asked him the next day. 'I have to know, to understand. You must not think me rude,' I begged, 'but I am in a mess myself and feel I am getting nowhere with my Freudian therapy.'

'Because I found I could not help some of my patients properly. Because I felt inside myself areas of illness not resolved by my Freudian analysis.'

And he started to explain how by treating troubled children, often only two or three, Mrs Klein had slowly forged an entirely new technique, which was based on her findings in the earliest infant mind. He added that in his own view and in his personal experience only this deepening grasp of the work which Freud began, could enable us to reach serious and early illness in our therapeutic task.

'So I should also change,' I asked, 'to a Kleinian analyst?'

'I was no longer in analysis. Changing can be difficult. It is you who must decide.'

As our small community achieved a certain modest name, it attracted now and then overseas psychiatrists wishing to be 'accredited' for the stipulated time required by our regulations. To my amazement, those who passed through our unit in this way had, without exception, come to do the Kleinian training here, at the London Institute. Like M, they all seemed willing to endure long separations from their home, and friends, and wider family, to learn here, in their promised land. They came from as far afield as Argentina and Brazil with all the twittering excitement of swallows homing to a well-loved nest. It was a stirring spectacle. My longings grew and multiplied. But I learnt that it can be easier to transplant oneself across whole worlds, than to find the courage it requires to terminate a therapy, with all the self-doubt that this

implies and the paranoid anxieties that are inevitably multipl
by such a unilateral step. I could not find a precedent for tl
particular divorce, however ardently I searched.

My Freudian psychotherapy was making little headway by this
time. We were yet again drearily bogged down in 'penis envy': that
atavistic panacea flogged by stagnant analysts, obstinately
unaware that those later grievances have a long prehistory in the
relationship of the infant to the breast. All my miseries, it seemed,
were due to being a mutilated male: dissatisfaction with a hidden
hole and withered penis substitute, even if none of this rang true in
terms of deep experience that clearly gloried in my breasts and
inner, fertile cavities, albeit secretly for fear of being called a witch.
But were these phallocentric views not being challenged from all
sides? There must be more to it than that. If I was envious, and I
was, I knew I envied everyone, women quite as much as men, who
found their own, creative paths and the domains to which these
lead: their secret garden on this earth, and the knowledge to make
it grow and flower, season by season, year by year – for as long as a
lifetime lasts.

This was a human privilege that was meant for either sex: for
sperm and ovum equally. I knew it in my inmost depths with an
age-old certainty, even if I could not risk saying it in so many
words. I could not yet speak my conviction for fear of being sent
away, while some furtive, secret part of me validated these
beliefs. Nevertheless, I could permit myself for the first time in my
life a wider use of library shelves to gather insights far afield,
risking the wrath of 'the grown-ups' with steadily mounting
confidence.

Slowly, through the weeks and months, this secret store of
insights grew towards an adequate critique of the trap that I was
in. And so all-powerful was this urge to forge the key to my chains
that I began to borrow books from my therapist's own shelves,
while he colluded in my quest. This was generous and kind. But
from a standpoint of technique it mirrored a catastrophe: for
by acceding to my wish, instead of analysing it, my Freudian
therapist confessed himself so far out of his depth that we now
required help from the lifeboats of the literature, seemingly by
joint consent.

In my diary there now appeared long quotations from these

works, as I burned the midnight oil engrossed in the travail of do-it-yourself analysis. If Freud had done it, why not I? And gradually the feeling grew that I had left RB behind, sadly lost and bemused, while I used every session to understand this growing wish to find a Kleinian analyst, though as yet I understood only the deep sense of frustration that my problems lay untouched, which drove me onwards in the dark. Still I was hoping fervently, praying might be a better word, that all this could be analysed to its neurotic origins, and my unrest could recede. Perhaps, I thought, I must accept that each conceptual edifice has its limitations. Or was I only splitting here: Kleinian 'good' and Freudian 'bad' with infantile omnipotence which I had begun to recognize. The thought of breaking off treatment filled me with horror, more and more.

A Kleinian analysis, in this guilty frame of mind, seemed like a fourth marriage after going through a third divorce, and I began to think of myself as a harpy, well beyond the pale. Yet the more ardently I stayed the course on that lonely Freudian couch, the more insistently did the imperative for change assert its urge from day to day with oracular monotony.

In February or March of that year, wearied by these diatribes, RB suggested that I ask the training body to agree to my much-desired change. A Kleinian analysis was still a Freudian one, he argued, so it could hardly be a crime. He seemed defeated, suddenly, ready to leave the battlefield; while far from feeling some relief I was simply terror-stricken to see this gentle warrior lay his empty rifle down. For with this gesture he confirmed my very worst anxieties, that I had drained and emptied him, so he was now about to die, which RB lamely countered with penis envy, yet again. The training body's answer was 'No'. God knows what their reasons were. Most likely, to be rid of me and my continual demands that the training be improved. But as far as I was now concerned the fat was really in the fire. I had the choice of battling on for a further eighteen months, if I wanted to obtain the benefits of membership of a professional body that would hopefully provide support in solitary and demanding work; or of being ejected into the cold, as I still saw it at the time. For in that dithery, dependent state I needed shelter to survive, while the other arguments were only rationalizations of that deeper, still unconscious trap.

What did my fellow students think?

'You ought to stick it out,' they said, 'now that you've got as far as this.' But most of them were timid souls. Social workers, in the main, they of course had to qualify, while as a doctor I could work as a psychotherapist without finishing the course. So was I going to drop out, or continue and 'belong'? I felt that I had never quite belonged to anything, or anywhere or anyone, and was longing to come in out of the cold at last. In this quandary there seemed no tunnel through or back door out. The stalemate appeared absolute when something happened, once again. I met a couple from New York, a professor and his wife who had brought their family to London a decade ago. In the States both had undergone Freudian analysis. Both had subsequently felt the need to have Kleinian help. I asked if I might come and have a quiet talk about it all.

Later, we became good friends. But on that evening, F sat and listened with an impassive face as I unburdened all my fears and uppermost anxieties. He then said drily that his own experience confirmed my views.

'But,' he concluded at the door, 'no one can tell you what to do. The final decision is your own.'

'I know,' I thanked him ruefully.

He did not try to clarify the issues for me in conceptual terms. Most probably he recognized that the confusions in my mind would only have been multiplied. But, in his generosity, he handed me on a slip of paper the name of his former analyst.

I had no way of knowing then what was to spring from this gift, that the name he had passed on to me was almost held in reverence in Kleinian circles throughout the world. And yet, as though half sensing this, I folded it most carefully, and kept it by me day and night, rather like a talisman, until its hour would arrive. That this would surely happen I never doubted in my heart of hearts. That winter night was dark and cold. But the evening had charged my battery when it seemed so low.

Spring returned. Easter found J, B, and myself on a holiday in Crete. The fishing village we had stumbled upon, off any beaten track, had no electricity. They offered us a little hut, an oil lamp and three simple beds: water from an old stone well drawn by a bucket on a chain. At night the men and women sat in a circle round the lamp of Kaliopi's smoke-filled bar. The kerosene threw greenish light on faces hewn out of Cretan rock. Dawn was heralded most days by the ticking diesel throb, as the wooden boats made home from the night's fishing fields, drawing shorewards one by one, while the eastern sky turned white, pink and orange and the sun strode across the purple peaks.

In the company of J, in this setting, gradually, my confused priorities underwent a subtle shift. What was a so-called 'training' that became a witch-hunt in this way? What was a psychotherapy that could not heal or clarify, that could not get near the roots of my genuine quest for help? In this location it was not possible to fool myself. The ritual of the daily task of this subsistence-living made 'expediency' a dirty word. If this community survived on so little, why must I let myself be paralysed by my insecurities? If they could face their nightly seas, why should I not face my own with that brand of steadfastness, despite the many differences that it was foolish to deny? And if these men and women could live and work here, side by side, through their ups and downs of life, then why could we not do the same, even if it seemed difficult and frightening in many ways to risk defeat another time. During those two weeks in Crete, J and I agreed we would resume our life as man and wife. Because in breaking up we had already lost our everything, there was nothing more to lose.

The sun grew stronger as the Greek Easter solemnly approached. In its little grassy patch, polka-dotted red and blue, yellow, crimson, white and mauve with the wild-flower life of spring, loud with the thrust of waves and bees and voices breaking into song, the village oven worked full-time. Batch after batch of Easter cakes, carried like small kings, aloft, were placed inside and then drawn out to the intoxicating scent of fresh-baked yeast and sea and smoke, of the smouldering olive wood that was fed in at the top, of wild thyme and marjoram, and the flowers of the orange trees in a dazzling April light. Then, many hours afterwards, the dark smell of the dying Christ, of incense and of candlewax, sorrow and tears: the smell of death. And, when midnight had arrived, the maddening rhythm of the bells: ding-ding-ding, ding-ding-ding, ding-ding, ding-ding, ding-ding, ding, as the small, packed Church grew dark, in this final night on earth, then candles, candles everywhere, and the bonfire set ablaze with Judas burned to mighty jeers and cheers to greet the risen Christ.

Back in London it was May. 'Only one more year to go,' my student friends encouraged me. I knew how deeply I would miss the warm and the consoling sense of student body membership, for the last time in my life. But I was not to be deterred in the decision I had made. Full of the sun and energy of Crete, full of the optimism that our marriage was to be repaired, clearly the moment had arrived to resume this odyssey of mine; to lift anchor once again and head for home.

But where is home, some part of me, the weary oarsman, muttered in revolt. How treacherously, in those days, the light of resolution still faded from my firmament. How waves spoke darkly in the tongues of sleep, on those drifting, schizoid seas. How Aurora faded grey on the daily London scene, the minute that new delays and frustrations blurred the way. For despite the new-found hope, the woman who returned from Crete in search of viability possessed no unitary existence yet; knew no beginning and saw no end, had no knowledge of her name, other than a distant call she had been taught to answer, as a sheepdog on the fells hears a master's whistle blow, signalling obedience.

A failure in her father's eyes, disaster on her mother's terms, she only recognized herself as two minus quantities still searching for a positive. For she had neither learnt the part of dazzling lady of the world, and consort of her father's dreams, nor had she managed the alternative which her mother might have recognized: that feminine excrescences should decently be sacrificed to minor, academic tasks until retirement and death offered a final, chaste reprieve.

Of this dark catastrophe – that on existential terms I was but two fantasias manqué – I only had the faintest knowledge, and merely sensed a prickly urge to peel some deadweight armour off, encasing me from top to toe, and watch what being might emerge, assuming it was still alive, somewhere in the inmost depths.

The first task that confronted me was the parting from RB, since it seemed devious to look for a Kleinian analyst while I was still seeing him, however tempting that might seem. But I was still quite unable to confront him face to face with the decision that I had reached with his support and patient help. Instead I pushed a little note through the old man's letter box, approaching that good house at dusk, and tearfully for the last time. Like that of an

111

outcast was my farewell to my Freudian therapist.

My sense of shock was deepened by the knowledge that I would be expelled from the training and the course, and by a growing certainty that dangerous months now stretched ahead. For the help I had received, as I acknowledged secretly, barred a facile swift return to euphoric states of mind that confront all guilt and pain with an omnipotent Hurrah, and get rid of deeper fear like so much ballast that no one wants.

That beautiful May evening, after our return from Crete, these considerations weighed heavily upon my heart. They also carried new relief since, as I recognized, they implied some new-found strength which a friendly parting from RB would have properly confirmed to my lasting benefit. However, through the coming weeks, I somehow managed to resist the temptation to withdraw to some island fantasy in my former, self-defeating ways, but struggled on to meet the demands of family life and of my job, as well as instituting the search for a Kleinian analyst.

However painful it was to stay in touch to this extent, for the first time in my life, with a hard core of reality, the reward for risking it was not very far behind. For no sooner could I keep vigil with my basic fears of coming totally unstuck, than support came from all sides: from my colleagues and from J, from the children and from different friends I hardly even knew I had. I now discovered that the world, when it is approached with trust, can offer us a true response, even if it takes some time to decode the offering. For it is different in kind from our infantile demands which are for instant, total care, or for swift re-entry to the womb by the very shortest route.

Now, supported on all sides, I followed the advice of F, given earlier in the year, and asked for an appointment with the name I had carried around with me since that cold, wintry night, and then awaited my great moment with such impatient spirit as Israel the voice of God.

He opened the front door himself, a giant from my childhood years. Decades in England had not touched the quiet reverence of a man who had lived among the mountains once. Even my disappointment that his small, partitioned waiting room, instead of looking over snowy peaks, lacked any window in its clean, white walls, could for the moment be contained by my restless Heidi mind. On the desk in his consulting room there stood prominently framed the photograph of a white-haired woman, a string of pearls around her neck, in curious contrast to her calm and composed austerity. Was it his mother, or his wife? Only later, when I bought Melanie Klein's Collected Works, did I recognize to whom that impressive face belonged.

I explained to Dr G that I was shortly moving back to J, and to the studio house, but that I also felt afraid. He asked me why and I replied: 'Something is wrong about that house. The studio is so large and light and all the rest is cramped and dark.'

'Just as you feel that all the light is only in the Institute, and you are outside in the dark.'

How had he guessed my constant pain that I was now too old to start training with the Institute, which I still regarded as the only true sanctuary of Freud? I marvelled at such genius since I was still some months away from any understanding of how I projected my own creativity into whoever lent themselves, for fear that I would be attacked by others if I showed a hint of talent, happiness or love. At the time, despite three psychotherapies, I had still not grasped the envious contortions of the mind, which Melanie Klein had clarified; and so I marvelled at how deeply he peered into my soul, when he hardly knew me yet. Before we parted, Dr G said that I would hear from him just as soon as he could find a Kleinian analyst who might offer me a vacancy.

June drifted on into July. Early July days staggered on, relentlessly, towards mid-month. People spoke of nothing but beaches, mountains, fjords and lakes. They rang like death knells in my ears. What was the use of aeroplanes, telephones and telegrams, first-class mail and hovercraft, when I was totally cut off on my barren rock of hate and old suspicions once again: my trust fragmented and my new hopes dashed by this interminable delay. Then almost unbelievably, he telephoned one evening in the last week of the month. My reeling senses hardly served to catch the name he offered me .'He is somebody whose work I think most highly of: rest assured.' Our contact ended with those words. I still remember vividly that anguish, felt in pantomimes, when the Good Fairy leaves the stage and we must hang on as best we can until her good spell comes to life. And yet I had no inner hands for hanging onto anything.

My Kleinian Home

The days before the interview, at the end of the same week, I thought and thought about those words. Up to now I had assumed that the person and the place of a psychoanalyst must be swathed in mysteries appropriate to the alchemists. The more the better, certainly. Precious metals, ornaments, symbols, halos, roots and herbs: I demanded everything, tutored properly by Jung, Hans Andersen and the Brothers Grimm. Now Dr G had scuttled that. It was the work, the actual work itself, that was significant. A thing that could presumably be evaluated and assessed like the ploughing and the crop.

This struck me as uniquely right and reassuring all at once. A breathtaking discovery, and I had made it just in time to shed some preconceived ideas which, disappointed, always led to withdrawal and hostility and a lot of acting out. It was certainly as well, because I was not going to find any trappings at this door. Even the window boxes had very little more than weeds.

The wooden plate above the bell of the simple garden flat spelt the surname: nothing more. No letters stood behind the name and no initials in the front. Not even 'Dr'. Not a hint.

The man himself seemed like his plate, simple, clear and to the point. He listened with attentiveness to everything I had to say: the years in Suffolk and the death of S, J's illness and my father's death, the training and the fiasco of my Freudian psychotherapy.

'So you have had quite a hard time.' The words came quietly and straight, as one might say, 'It rained last night.'

'Yes,' I said, 'it has been hard.'

The simple, unaffected phrase emerged as an immense relief. I was no more compelled to play 'not really', with a manic shrug. The edifice of my false pride and boundless grandiosity had been laid bare to some degree, however rudimentary. This meant that I could at long last admit, with some directness, that I had come out of the deepest need of my own necessity and out of a growing certainty of how badly I would need his help.

'Perhaps you found it difficult that your previous analyst was not Jewish,' he now said.

No sooner had I looked at him in the light of these bland words, than I could clearly recognize that SK was Jewish, like myself, and also that the purpose of these words was to make very clear both the acknowledgement that I had certain grounds for pain, and that after this we would eschew every witch-hunt of RB.

'Yes, that was very difficult . . . '

I rather wanted to enlarge on my list of grievances and RB's shortcomings at once, to air them in my usual way, but glancing at that tranquil face I desisted, since I felt ashamed and suddenly very guilty in the silence that ensued.

'I shall give you an awful time . . . I fear.' I said the words dejectedly, on the sudden brink of tears, thinking of poor RB again, how I had hurt him endlessly.

'That is alright,' came the reply. He did not toss my words aside, nor seem to waver at their sound.

With his three words SK replied that he was up to it all right, that he could take whatever came. An instant insight had been used to allay a wild anxiety, with which I would have otherwise been stranded through the holidays: that I was bound to prove too much for any analyst on earth and beyond the reach of help. Today I recognize the height of psychotherapeutic skill in interventions of this kind. But at the time I only sensed some dream-like measure of relief, being still a stranger to my inner life, with its fragile and subtle filigree of a sea-anemone that stirs in opalescent depths with currents that no eye can see. All that remained was to agree the details about times and fees, and leave the quiet garden flat with the lightest of hearts.

Around that time I had a dream. A poor and wasted garden in my care was dug up wildly here and there where some canes or bushes bore an early crop of some precarious fruit; but for the most part it was still a dusty, stubborn wilderness. The dream appeared to be connected with the Suffolk garden we had had. With its ancient, sombre trees, flanked by fields of rolling grain,

115

that tangled wilderness had seemed past reclaiming we had feared, and several decent gardeners had been defeated in a row. Only when Mr Taylor came and looked at the impoverished soil, that lay like so much ash and dust in his outstretched palm, and after a long silence said: 'Will you bear with me, just yet, if I need to take my time and put some food in this old soil, that is neglected something cruel,' did we recognize that here was the gardener for us. And within several years a garden gladdened every eye that rested on the old, grey house.

Some days after that interview I moved myself and all I had back into J's studio house. I now felt sure that a life to call one's very own could be achieved under a husband's roof as well as under any other sort. But I had never liked the house, nor the surrounding area. There were no gardens and no trees. A busy bus route in the front, six lanes of clearway at the rear, screened only slightly by two streets that the developers had left, with traffic sweeping day and night to Heathrow and the mines of Wales, all of which only echoed my inner restlessness.

As people often do I rationalized these deeper fears: where was B now going to play with some degree of safety? Where would she ride her bicycle? Would D accept the uproar who had so much studying to do for Cambridge entrance? These worries proved superfluous since they were mainly rooted in class prejudices that I then still felt duty-bound to share, as Mother's good, obedient girl.

J was wonderfully above all snobbery about a house, as long as it provided him with a studio to meet his needs, in terms of floorspace, height and light: a tall order in the urban scene – all of which requirements the London studio fulfilled. The rest was quite irrelevant as far as he was concerned. Nonetheless, once I was back, he was willing to concede to my solidly entrenched bourgeois sensibilities, even if they baffled him.

When we married, well before London somewhat sad but wise became a smokeless zone, we had shared our living space with two enormous Pither's stoves: one in the studio, one upstairs in our kitchen-living-room. Romantically we had loved these dusty monsters at the time and tended them with little thought for the dirt and bother this entailed. But now a modern age had come and men had landed on the moon! J could not really see the point. His mother, who took washing in, had carried water in a pail. But since, out of some wild caprice, my heart seemed set on better things, he was prepared to see them through, and in the coming weeks endured with heroic fortitude a home disrupted blow by blow by central heating engineers and decorators. It was a loving sacrifice from one who values peace and quiet above everything on earth and helped me find the peace of mind I urgently required now, to settle down and sink my roots into what would, through the years, grow to be my Kleinian home.

Yet when the longed-for day to start the analysis arrived, I realized to my pain and grief that I was now confronted by a new disaster: it was that I had simply no idea of *how* I was to settle down when it really came to it. Though everything had been agreed, before the summer holiday, my deeper mind seemed to rebel. Come to this room *five* times a week? Lie still and quiet on the couch? The notion seemed preposterous! Why could I not sit on the floor? Why could we both not take a walk into the garden, through the nice French door? Roses bloomed in profusion still, as autumn lingered on and on. I wanted us to run and play. To find a sand-pit and a swing.

'You do not like restriction, then?' the voice behind me said each day.

Restriction was intolerable! Restriction that meant staying still – and missing 'all those lovely things'; and risking . . . what? I did not know. I would discover presently. All I knew was that I must be free to up and run and run and run.

The need to flee for my dear life seemed so imperious at first that I could not even hear the words that SK said to me: 'I'm sorry. But I cannot hear.' My panic mounted. Was I deaf? How could I have analysis? How was I going to be helped?

'It seems you cannot take them in, these words that I am giving you.'

What was the use of telling me? Was it not terrible enough? And then, when the first Friday came, I spoke of nothing except death and dangerous roads and accidents.

'You feel you cannot bring me back.'

'I cannot. Yes. I know, but why?'

'Perhaps you feel you do not have enough good feelings to bring me back.'

To bring him back when Monday came? Yes, he was absolutely

right! If it seemed strange and even mad, it still rung true, beyond all doubt.

My old, wild-life intolerance to all restrictions, that was hardly news, though I had never questioned it before, since I assumed that everyone needed above all to be 'free', which I believed meant unrestrained. But this latest shock hit me like a revelation: what *did* I have to bring him back? Nothing, my hollow being raged. Nothing. You have not anything. You are doomed and might as well be dead.

On that first Friday afternoon, before the first of many separations struck, I lay there paralysed and cold with this appalling sense of emptiness – though it was only the first taste – of having nothing of my own, nothing of value, nothing good to offer him to bring him back; to bring his big, green Volvo back to its allocated place: no resources of my own. So now he had me, the mean rogue, exactly where he wanted me, helpless at his beck and call. My hopes and dreams had ended here and now in this disgusting trap.

'You feel that you do not possess inner resources of your own.' I staggered blindly from the room. I had no way of knowing yet how painfully I hated him each time he left me, or that separation meant that I was surely bound to die of starvation and neglect.

Out in the sunshine of the street, the awful feeling quickly passed. Perhaps I had imagined it. It seemed ricidulous. Absurd. I had a house, a family, profession, patients – everything. I was not bankrupt. He was mad. Not to be trusted an inch! That a baby part of me raged in total disregard of these fine realities, I would discover presently.

When Monday came, I was amazed to see the Volvo standing there. So he had come back after all. No tricks. He hadn't run away. I said it seemed a great relief.

'So you had not expected it.'

'Not altogether,' and I laughed. It all seemed childish, beyond words.

In all my previous therapies I watched the time, a little bored, while keeping carefully aloof, but this was something different.

'I think I've lost my appetite.'

'You are afraid,' the answer came, 'of getting too much out of it.'

Ridiculous. But it was true.

'What am I getting, though?' I sighed.

'Perhaps you're very frightened of a greedy part, inside yourself? Afraid, that if you come too close, you're going to lose yourself in me.' It was entirely true again, however strange the words might seem. For months I was to battle with a fantasy of getting stuck: getting inside and never out, or of somehow merging with SK. I kept remembering how Pooh had too many elevenses and then got stuck in Rabbit's hole. That danger never left my mind. The fact that Pooh Bear represented a guzzling baby-part of me, that felt it was insatiable, still lay outside my mental reach.

'You also want to lose yourself.' But that came many months afterwards, and then I marvelled at the skill that he had waited with this one. For, had he said it at the start, I might have fled and not come back.

Such things are better not looked at before we are sufficiently of one piece: before the Ego has begun to stand on its own two feet, instead of splitting constantly, even fragmenting totally, as mine would do in self-defence the very minute that I felt even remotely criticized – less than perfect or marvellous. Eventually I reached the stage where I could feel my fragile Ego breaking with such clarity that I imagined I could count how many fragments this time round: two, three, or had the whole lot gone, each time that I attacked myself for finding something that was 'wrong', and spoilt my lovely self-image, as I gazed into that pond of poor Narcissus, who was all alone. For months and years I was afraid I couldn't bear one further truth and face how 'horrible' I was: greedy and mean and hideous – ordinary, in other words. Much like everybody else. Not the saint I thought I was.

But gradually these fears wore off and I could start to concentrate a little better on SK and on the whole analysis. Slowly the fear of getting lost, or of getting stuck, diminished and with its fading, gradually, a sense of timelessness began; and an immense excitement grew, despite the set-backs steadily, until I came to recognize that I had waited all my life for this incredible reprieve of finding all the missing links and words and switches in the dark where I had lain hiding; this prince had come at last, although I still devalued him, suspicious of what he might be up to. Also, along with this relief came an overwhelming guilt: that by being here, day after day, I was displacing someone else. If I was *in*,

119

someone was *out*. There wasn't room for everyone, for all the children in the world. How could there be sufficient food? Now all the others had to starve and watch my feast with envious eyes: the lucky baby at the breast.

Mother had been denied this help. And J. And everyone I loved. I'd had my share. I'd had enough. Now it was someone else's turn. Perhaps my brother ought to come with all the problems that he had. I'd go and fetch him and then leave.

Time and again this guilt returned that I was getting much too much. The same fear back and back again. Whenever it appeared resolved, there it was again: back once more and still more painful each time round as my capacity to feel joy and sorrow slowly grew: a first small appetite for life and love. How I longed to share it out, make them all better, to repair the world, to mend the damage that I felt I'd caused. Oh, I had broken everyone. How could I start to make them whole? The pain seemed unendurable. Often I simply longed to have my thick skin back again, to undo everything I'd gained. Give it to others who had need. Why should I have this benefit. It seemed entirely undeserved.

This Good, at first, still lacked a name. Only as the years went by I knew that it was sanity. Of such possessions as I own, it is the one I value most. After such years of poverty, of hungering in the twisted dark, it is the wealth that really counts, that nobody can take away, provided we devote ourselves to its upkeep steadfastly.

'You are afraid,' SK would say, 'of being better off than someone else.' Yes, I was really terrified. For then, what would they do to me?

That we were tackling envy now, and in particular the envy which insight and understanding arouse, I only realized afterwards. With so much skill, SK had undercut the intellectualizing that I had so far always used as a first line of defence. With his choice of simple words he took that ground from under me without which the analysis might well have run onto the rocks of studious sterility. For we can all use cleverness as so much extraneous froth in which self-alienation grows to strangle feeling at the roots.

Once envy lessened, gradually I found that I could write again, although the knack had seemed all but lost through many dreary, empty months.

All very nice and very well. But now the fears came crowding back: all this was stolen from SK. If I took more and more he would shrivel up and die. There would be nothing, nothing left of my Kleinian analyst, if I was getting such a lot, taking all this 'out of him', as my concrete thinking ran again.

Friday after Friday I still spoke of little but catastrophe. Friday after Friday we explored the old conviction that I had nothing at all to offer him: nothing with which to bring him back. My casework was improving now. The poetry was flowing back, on paper, and in life itself; but I had nothing, not a thing, by deep conviction and experience, on which our self-esteem might rest.

'You are afraid,' SK would say, 'that you will get no more support, if you acknowledge what you have.'

So month by month we battled on. Each Monday I remained amazed to find he'd come back after all: to see that he was there again, unlike my father in the past. But Mondays remained terrible. A weekend load of grievances. Everyone had let me down. Stories of people I had known who had abandoned little pets. Children who had been put in homes. Week after week I could not feel the fury towards poor SK for leaving me when Friday came. Patiently he stood his ground. Week after week he pointed out that in my fantasies I felt deprived of resources in myself with which I could sustain my life. That I lacked confidence in these or the belief that they might grow: that anything would ever change.

Nonetheless, I was by now gradually starting to believe in my good feelings, here and there, though quite unsteadily as yet. Like a loose contact in a bulb, they flickered wildly off and on. On in the middle of the week and dying out towards the end. Then, when a rudimentary belief in my own inner scaffolding emerged, I felt that if I relied on it I would use the very structure up and then depend on the supplies SK still brought from day to day, until there would be nothing left. And yet, each Monday he came back, prepared to run the awful risk of being emptied and drained. Where was the catch in all of this, I pondered intermittently, instantly suspicious despite the progess that was being made.

With this conflict to the front, Friday had by now become disaster area number one. The world itself came to an end. Home, after a dreadful drive through dark, empty, dangerous streets, where death was lurking everywhere, after a first aid cup of tea, I would crawl forsaken into bed. Was that not what my patients did in the unit dormitory, spend their entire lives in bed? And was I not turning into that: complete disfunction, week by week? Whatever would my family think?

But B, it seemed, could understand. When she had returned from school, sometimes, on Fridays, she would bring me her enormous teddy bear, her remedy for all life's ills, and I would take it, half-ashamed, pretending it was just a game, and drift into a welcome sleep, withdrawing from the pains of life: of separation from SK.

During this seemingly endless stage, I once asked M, in near despair, whether I would never stop howling for my analyst when the weekend came.

'Excellent patient,' M replied with a hidden little smile. I asked myself whether he also howled and all the other colleagues too? I was too scared to ask them, though. I was afraid to get the sack. Yet even as I felt myself sliding downhill in the worst landslide I had ever known any regression to assume, came the first glimmerings of trust: that possibly, just possibly, SK knew what he was about.

But hardly had I just begun to feel this little scrap of trust under my weary feet, when it all caved in again: he would lead me up the garden path and then walk out and simply nevermore come back. Hadn't my father done just that? And, for the sake of argument, assuming that SK would not, that he was made of firmer stuff, would not the world pull us apart? Did it not endlessly throw up cataclysms of all sorts, like Hitler, revolutions, total war: all that had carried Father off, whether he wanted it or not. Were we not after all helpless beings, torn apart, despite the best will in the world to stay together? And what could the English-born SK know of such catastrophes? I hear the words I flung at him. This time, I felt, I had him floored. There was no answer to that! Was that not history itself, and wholly incontestable? And very quietly the voice, when my raving had died down: 'There is such a thing as living in constant expectation of disaster coming from within.' It seemed to make some deeper sense. Or was he just consoling me?

I could not have realized at this stage, nor yet for many months to come, that the most frightening thought of all was that I could trust my analyst. For does not a world where there is trust ask a great deal in return? Where would I find the wherewithal? How could I possibly fulfil such expectations and demands? Besides, if I could really trust, the fear that he would one day die would surely prove unbearable? No, I could not cope with that. Although I did not know it then, my Ego still lacked the strength to bear such deep anxieties. So it was safer not to trust, care very deeply or to love. That was still a long way off.

So fresh suspicions now appeared to spoil this possibility. I grew convinced that SK hid dolly-birds here in the flat. Who in his right mind kept a flat a stone's throw from his private home, just for seeing patients in? Certainly he kept the place for dubious liaisons of all kinds. Had not these apparitions drifted into my father's flat, perfumed, slinky, elegant, every time we visited? Nor had they come through the front door, like my small brother and myself, when our chauffeur rang the bell. No bell to warn of *their* approach. Snakes in the grass of memory hissed; and evidently this took place because I was not good enough, or nice or beautiful enough, and because I lacked whatever I lacked here and now, or SK would not go away and leave me each time Friday came, but take me with him everywhere.

'You do not value yourself,' said the voice, from behind me on the couch, with endless patience, day by day, Monday by Monday and of course, on those bleak Fridays most of all.

None of my previous analysts had ever mentioned this before, this paramount and obvious fact. If my father, long ago, had found so little time for me, before he disappeared; and if my mother had kept me in a nursery, which even had a padded door – it proved that I had little worth. Noisy, nasty, tiresome, a disappointment to them both. Very probably SK was sorry he had me too, and any day now he'd engage a starchy nanny in his place to see to my immense demands, my anger and destructive ways. I was too much for anyone. The past had proved it, beyond doubt. But what was very, very strange was that he kept on coming back. Always he was there himself. No nanny ever came instead.

True, other patients sometimes came. At times, when it was my turn, I had to sit 'outside' and wait, straining to catch those sounds within. At others, when I'd been 'inside', a 'boy' or 'girl' sat waiting there. A coat, a jacket or a bag in the little entrance hall caused instant panic in my soul. All this was further evidence of how disappointing I must be, or he would spend all his time with me and not want anybody else. Why should I share him, anyway?

I started to complain of mice. 'The other children Mother had,' the comment from behind me came. My little brother must have come because I had disappointed them. If I had been a *lovely* girl, why should my parents have desired another baby after me? If I had any value now, why would SK not leave his wife, his children, all his family and dedicate his life to me? My pet aversion soon became a patient who looked Japanese who, when he came, would ring the bell while I was lying on the couch, although the door was always on the latch to obviate the need for giving me such horrid jolts. Unable to contain my rage I was extremely rude to him.

On the couch, the following day, I speculated angrily why this foreign monster had all those murderous fantasies to have to warn of his approach. It was a shock when I found out those murderous feelings were my own where any rival was concerned: a little brother worst of all. Nor was he even Japanese. But my associations flew to hara-kiri, and from there to early photo-portraits of myself: just like a small doll from Japan. Putting the two together next, it struck me with a dreadful grief, how after my small brother's birth I had transformed myself into this trying-to-please-you-please, solemn, wooden little doll, committing hara-kiri where my deeper feelings were concerned.

Next time the 'monster' was outside, I managed to apologize. Nor did he ring the bell again. Doubtless, he had also dealt with fantasies about me. Many months afterwards we met. He was a child psychiatrist and we could share a heartfelt laugh.

Now I was coming to suspect that I depended on SK. That not only was he a dumping ground for day-to-day anxieties, but that he nourished me in endless ways I could no longer do without. Then the risk of losing him reached panic stations; and by that very token still obliged me to devalue him, to save myself, as I assumed, from the shattering grief of later loss. The more my loving feelings grew the more I mocked him, day by day. He was no artist; not like J. He had no studio, big and light, only this little garden flat: a poor conversion job at that, which leaked whenever it rained hard.

Until the leak could be repaired he had, at times, to interrupt a session briefly to put towels over the desk and on the floor. I lay and watched this brief redress, filled with the most despairing pain to think my father had not once tended to my safety or small-girl well-being in such ways. Instead, immaculately dressed, Father had always fended off sticky attempts to come too close, as I was fending off the risk of coming closer to SK. For in that case I would be lost, taken over – disappear. My fragile Ego boundaries would simply melt down and dissolve, at which point he would suck me in, as my unconscious terrors ran.

So, panic-stricken by each sign that trust and love were slowly closing in, I used my psychoanalytic jargon to try and keep him at arm's length and prove that I could help myself from other sources, if need be. Do-it-yourself analysis, as I had evolved it with RB, returned with due monotony. And rather than entrust myself to my hard-won analyst, now that I had him finally, I ran to authors like Kohut, and started spouting by the page in my precious minutes on the couch on the 'Narcissistic Personality and its Defence by Arrogance'. Close to the mark and yet so far!

This time I had met my master, though. And thanks to that there came a day when I was made to recognize the armour plating of my own devastating arrogance, welded against helplessness, in which I drove my endlessly growing love endlessly into the ground, session by session, week by week, and given even half a chance, very likely year by year. This meant that I now had to face the guilt, self-hatred and despair at my conduct in the past, yet sensing with huge relief that this meant I was strong enough to bear the burden of my guilt. This anguish spelt a victory on the slow and uphill road of casting all the devils out. But how should one convey such love? If I gave the game away, would the seducer not take advantage of me and walk out on me?

I think I rather hoped he would and then, before it was too late, before I was committed, I would triumph, jeer and crow: ha, it is nothing after all except the oldest con trick on this earth, like Mother and like Father: here one minute, gone the next. Hollow pretence and little more: words, empty words to conjure with, or to appease a weepy child.

So week by week we battled on. I would come closer and withdraw, like fallow deer at dusk and dawn. Wednesdays and Thursdays I came close. Fridays, I turned tail and ran. Mondays would be pretty angry, on the whole, although less angry than before. Less chock-a-block with grievances. Then, finally, came a milestone. Halfway to Easter, after six or seven months of solid work, I moaned one day despairingly: 'How can I say I love you if to say it frightens me so much?'

'But you just said it,' said SK in his quiet, level voice, although he must have recognized the breakthrough we had just achieved.

It was to prove a turning point. But for the help of earlier analysis, it might have taken further years, considering how ill I was, although I still lacked all idea of the frightening extent of my emotional handicaps.

But despite this cosy interlude, the black clouds of the approaching Easter break were drawing in, as hate and rage surged uppermost and I started to withdraw, in the old, defensive way. Had I not been obedient? Worked hard to please him, endlessly? Swallowed his nasty medicine of awful and at times even positively humiliating interpretations day by day with little murmur or revolt? So why should he be off again? Would someone kindly tell me why, and just what might be wrong with me?

At Easter we were back in Crete. I missed him and felt desolate. Only my writing eased the pain through two long weeks of banishment, although another part of me took pleasure in the holiday and let the mountains, sun and sea break through my longings as through mist. Then all was swallowed up again as a deep depression grew and seemed to gain the upper hand.

Despite this longing for SK, it was not easy coming back. On the return flight, high above the Mont Blanc chain of icy peaks like a Yeti's teeth below, the thought had shivered through my blood: my life lay in the pilot's hands. Never had I let that truth even cross my mind before, veteran traveller that I was. And hardly had I told SK, than I knew the meaning for myself, in deeper terms of here and now of my deep dependency, even though the destructive feelings were back in the ascendancy for the beginning of the summer term.

But now there was a part of me that stood increasingly aside and questioned the old grievances that he kept on 'going off'. Instead, I came to see and feel the steadfastness of the concern that I received five times a week, even if it was not the non-stop care for which the infant-me still screamed. Gradually, in other words, I became less insatiable, as I began to recognize that I had resources of my own that I could depend and draw upon; and that no one was going to feel rejected as a consequence, the way I felt each time SK showed signs of living his own life at weekends and the holidays. The very thing I could not do, because I felt I must fit in with what others might demand, or else they would get rid of me. In other words, if I could put my weekends to creative use, wouldn't that mean the end of my analysis: 'new babies' waiting to be born, long before I had been weaned?

In this connection, I now saw, I had absconded from RB in the May of our second year: the month my brother had been born, just after I myself was two, rather than have to face again the old, anticipated pain of having to discover a new baby in my mother's arms. My mother, who belonged to me, whom I would never, never share.

Nevertheless, no matter what mischief kept on welling up out of the unconscious mind, nothing ever seemed as bad, or quite as desolate again, once I had confessed my love and felt it was accepted with reciprocity and warmth as a matter of course and an indication of the progess we had made. Now, like a lighthouse it stood firm, regardless of recurring storms, and let me navigate a safe return from the seas of rage and helplessness. I began to learn to steer between the rocks of hate and envy, of aggression and despair, as these in turn shrank out of sight.

They seemed mere sandbanks, I believed, as we drew closer to the summer break. Five weeks, why should I be afraid? Was I not able, as I now believed, to guard the good that was in me, or reinstate it every time that I had battered it again in moments of despondency? Had I not come to understand that everything that 'happened' to me in the quotidian 'outer' world only reflected how my 'inner' one was at that moment taking care of my 'inner' analyst? That all the trivia of the daily round, that seemed so ominous at times, were generally little more than a running commentary on that innermost dialogue, between the baby and the breast that went so wrong the first time round and from which my difficulties stemmed? And now that summer had arrived, and he deserved his holiday, was there a reason on this earth why I should not run along and lose myself in happy play, quite safe and certain that he would be back on the appointed day?

It had been very hard for me to reach this outpost of preliminary trust. In the very earliest months, to my absolute dismay, I turned him out in half an hour; so by the time that I reached home I'd lost my analyst again, to emptiness and hungry rage, for the rest of the weekend. Then followed anxious winter months, when I would waken in the night to search for SK in my heart, with feverish anxiety, to find him missing, once again; when I would simply have to wait in abysmal helplessness for Monday's session to work out what anger or anxiety, mistrust or insecurity had made me cast him out once more.

But slowly spring had come along and with it, warmer summer months, when I no longer had to try that rather frightening exercise. I simply knew that he was there, just as I would not need to check my fingers, muscles or my bones. Then why fear five short summer weeks? What seas could make me lose that beacon by which I sailed my ship as sailors do by the stars at night?

But I had not quite bargained for an angry infant still entrenched in some recesses of my dread about surviving on my own. I could now hold onto my love, but lacked the faith that it could co-exist with all the anger in my heart. And so there seemed no option but to turn that hate against myself. I ended up in hospital strung to an ECG machine, for palpitations that became quite severe at intervals.

'It's only separation pains. Nothing the matter with my heart, despite what your pictures say.'

The tears were streaming down my face. The tracing seemed quite ominous. My colleagues stood and shook their heads, as, regardless of their advice, I put my clothes on and went home to await SK's return.

When that reunion day arrived: 'I nearly died', I hurled at him. And then I simply lay and wept, session by session, week after week.

'Why on earth did you not know of all the trouble I was in? Beastly man, you should have come to that awful hospital and made me better straight away. My heart would sometimes stop so long, I felt that if you did not come it would not ever start again. You left me, just like Nanny did.'

For two long weeks I raged and raged. What was the use of loving him, when, in the end, we had to part? Had my father waited till I was ready and grown up? No, he had married someone else.

SK would never leave his wife, when I was ready in the end: selfish and cold-hearted man, my Oedipal frustrations raged. But hand in hand with these renewed onslaughts on my patient analyst, went a deepening belief that we would weather all these storms, that our good feelings would prevail and that my love could make repair however great the damage done.

As this belief grew month by month, I was able to observe from within its sheltering arms, how I used the sledgehammer of my ever-present hate to splinter myself yet again. Lying safely on the couch, I could see the many pieces scattered far and wide as if a bomb had just gone off within a hair's breadth of my life, each time I made some slight mistake.

Slowly, I came to understand how sternly my conscience treated me; as savage as the ancient gods. But once I saw this, it began to change. I learnt how to forgive myself, however long that process took, for the kind of daily blunders we all make. As psychoanalysts would say, my 'Super-ego' grew 'less harsh' and very much less punishing. And with this change, my resolve grew to come together and repair not only others but also myself, as the leaves came down for the second autumn term into the garden that I loved so well. My new security, as I myself began to sense, was growing from the depths of early wounds and unresolved anxieties. This work in progress, I now felt, would leave no big, untidy gaps to fester stealthily beneath the healing process which inched on, despite the setbacks strewn along the path of each analysis. Certainly, I was to find that setbacks and resistances were always hovering in the wings: an inbuilt opposition since the mind so readily attacks its highest purpose: consciousness. At times it seemed that every pain brought along its twin retreat. Hardly, for instance, did I seem to enjoy my weekends than this liberation brought fresh fears to the relentless light of day. If I could invest my time in happy productivity and be creative in those hours, as well as in our session time; if, in other words, I stopped swallowing SK's every word like an obedient little girl and brought ideas that were my own into the analysis, then would he not like Rumpelstiltskin, or my mother long ago, stamp his foot and fly away in total rage for ever more? Could he really tolerate my version of being simply me – meaning different from himself – or would he, in the bitter end, attack the progress I had made, my bid for real

129

autonomy, and prove a mother who could not, for all the lipservice she paid, bear her daughter growing up to find her own, intrinsic ways? And was I able, on my part, to see this process that was under way as a loving reciprocity instead of heady cleverness stolen from my analyst and furtively absconded with at every opportunity. In that case it would represent a hostile triumph once again, dependency would be denied, while such ground would never let the true seed germinate and thrive, but turn into the deadly soil of mania with its cold contempt and its recurring scuttling of innermost reality.

Day by day this ground was dug and cleared of the decades of weeds whose roots seemed everywhere and always ready to return, like those convoluted strings the ground elder will always drag such distance from the actual plant. And as that waste was slowly cleared to resemble honest earth, I was able presently for the first time in my life, to approach and be approached by other beings like myself, with the same weaknesses and strengths, same fears and longings, joys and griefs.

Slowly, very stealthily, like a small, wild animal, I started risking step by step to advance from the psychotic cold and isolation of the past, from the lonely hateful void, towards the fires of my kind, and a life that could be shared. True, such contacts still remained a bit unsteady, even loose at times. There would be sessions with SK when the light still flickered in the old, wild way of wholesale infidelity. Or I would totally withdraw into that drowsy non-chalance that is the hallmark of the schizoid mind, as fresh anxieties sprang up, or different aspects of the older ones sneaked in, in unfamiliar disguises along the spiral of this awesome task. How easily this is the case. Does not being human mean losing each other now and then? Did Christ, before he died, not doubt? Which of the famous cries came first? Even the Scriptures disagree! Surprising as these kinships seem, these are the issues that now link our Kleinian concepts with time-honoured ones in our latest healing work.

As the analysis proceeded, I saw more closely how every imagined cause for cutting myself off again could prove remedial in the context of our deepening contact and my growing trust. Nevertheless, I was to find, these were still the early days of a deep analysis. For even if I had achieved a modicum of trust and love I knew I was quite powerless when it came to holding onto it, as the third year now disclosed.

All very well to love SK, when I was with him and 'inside', as in a mother, still unborn, nice and cosy, warm and safe in the symbiotic caul – but what if I had to be outside? If I must presently be born and fight for air and food and warmth and very likely not survive unless he took the utmost care and stayed with me continuously? Contemplating such a pass, my dependence now seemed so abject and so absolute, my helplessness so terrible, that we were very shortly back to the beginning, as it seemed. Weekends that had just about seemed a little bearable, became wild and dangerous ground again. Love was hardly to be seen, for it had been conditional on being allowed to live 'inside' and fight to keep all others out: Father, babies and the lot. I loved, provided I could own, keep sole possession, and control the situation with absolute omnipotence. Every alternative seemed fraught with risks that seemed a threat to life itself.

So, in the following months, I had to re-establish whether my resources would suffice once I consented to be born and so be separate from SK, or whether I was going to starve and die the • minute that he went away. I was a doctor, certainly, but in terms of baby-dread, I seemed determined not to yield to such sops from 'mere' reality. This brought about a constant fear that if I showed the slightest hint of my real capacities, SK would drop me instantly and a new baby would be born. Had it not happened once before, the very minute I could walk across the nursery in Berlin?

So deeply rooted was this fear in earlier experience, that I took the utmost care to conceal from both of us that I could manage anything whatsoever on my own. This baffling sense of helplessness seemed to persist endlessly. I feared all progress had been lost and that I was heading backwards to some pre-existent vegetable, or blind and senseless embryo. The instant that I felt alive or took some small initiative, an inner shutter rattled down and all became dark and still again in the sickroom of my life. It was halfway through the summer term of the second analytic year when the following took place.

It was a beautiful weekend and J decided we would spend Sunday in Sussex with some friends. The sun shone from a cloudless sky. We broke the journey where a sign said: pick your

131

own strawberries. The strawberry fields lay at the foot of the South Downs where they basked between us and the open sea. The South Downs of my Bedales time that I had not seen for years! A surge of happiness broke through the woolly blanket of my fears. To my utter disbelief, I felt a surge of joyous life. How could I have forgotten that the world could be so beautiful? How was it possible to have mislaid these glowing images? We stopped for morning coffee at a small, inviting coffee shop. Lupins and campanulae, roses, pansies and marigolds looped around small tables set on a gentle English lawn. Sussex greeted me unchanged, like a dear, familiar face.

Our friend, a painter, gave us lunch. Afterwards we wandered past Monk's House, the former home of Leonard and Virginia Woolf, and since nobody seemed around, through the little wooden gate into the garden bathed in light. I felt that I could run and run; who knows, but perhaps I could even fly. It was with great reluctance that I finally agreed to leave this enchanted Sussex realm, back to my London life that now felt strangely burdensome and remote from earlier, carefree happiness.

With only twenty minutes to go, the traffic thickened morbidly. Slowly I began to feel very anxious, strange, unreal: that I was going to collapse. I pulled the car up on a verge and cold with terror took my pulse. It raced too fast for me to count. Now everything was going dark. Surely, I was dying of an internal haemorrhage. Soon an ambulance arrived and swept all three of us away to the local hospital. No, they did not think it was any kind of haemorrhage. More probably a heart attack. The ECG was very queer. No, it was not a coronary. There was no knowing what it was.

By Monday it had dawned on me that the entire episode, in all its unreality, would be better analysed, and like a life-long invalid I took a taxi to SK. There, it presently grew clear how deeply guilty I had felt at this burst of happiness and brief display of liveliness. That it was not really mine, but stolen from my analyst in a hostile, treacherous way, to leave him plundered, doomed to die. The carefree well-being had turned to a manic triumph in which I felt I did not need him any more if I myself was full of life; then feared he would retaliate as soon as London came in sight and with it the analysis on Monday.

For months afterwards I could hardly bear to drive. For whenever I put distance of any consequence between my analyst and myself, stretching out an imaginary cord that bound me to him for supplies, I promptly started to feel faint.

Slowly, I began to see how simply terrified I was to make the very smallest move, be it in body or in thought, that was spontaneous and my own. Any idea that came from me threatened a mother who desired to exert complete control and simply would not tolerate any sign of separate life or independence on my part; or else she would get rid of me and cut me off from the supplies upon which, in fantasy, I still felt I depended in this symbiotic trap. Only now did I begin to understand that these fearful fantasies which we gradually unearthed were partly a reversal of my own intentions to control every move this mother made, with a relentless, iron will. The fight was to keep her for myself, away from the father who would take my cosy, rightful place inside that we were both competing for. If I gave him half a chance, not only would he steal my nest, but further babies would be born and displace me totally.

Since sadly, in reality, my 'outer' mother lent herself to these possessive fantasies, to the fears that she would never let me live a life that was my own, I had long ago acquired an 'inner' mother who applied the brakes to every move I made to cut the symbiotic bonds. Part of my inner world, this anti-life, forbidding witch, who crippled my attempts to live, was, in the analysis, projected into my analyst, who I felt would withdraw support the minute that I made a bid for freedom and autonomy.

Slowly I began to see the classic schizophrenic trap whose life-long prisoner I had been. But understanding could at first not change unconscious strategies that were so solidly entrenched. Nevertheless, we inched ahead. At weekends and during holidays I was still quite paralysed with terror of impending doom. I fought these fears determinedly, but nobody was quite deceived. Whether we were in Greece or Spain I struggled through the holidays of the first three analytic years quite certain that the separation was bound to be the end of me. It was hard on all of us, but never once did J complain.

But despite the suffering, the urge to see it through remained. And once I had begun to see more clearly that its purpose was to create an entity that could separate from SK, very slowly more and

133

more of my personality came over from the enemy lines of the illness to the side of this thrust for hope and life.

After two years with SK and the fourth year of my job at the mental hospital, the longing grew to work at home and treat patients of my own for longer periods and in greater depth than it was possible to do in the Unit where I worked. At the same time I felt terrified of giving safe employment up: that semblance of security which grows into a life-long trap, preventing us from using our initiative and trusting in our gifts and skill in so many walks of life.

'But where would I get patients from?' I kept repeating on the couch.

'You don't trust your resources yet. You do not feel that you have had sufficient help from me, it seems.'

I thought about this and could feel how I persisted in getting rid of all the insights that I had received because a part of me still craved exclusive and continuous care as evidence of real concern. If that was going to be withheld then I would simply throw away the good help that was given me. Hey presto, it was just expelled and flushed away like excrement to leave me empty as before: cold and needy and deprived.

Gradually my courage grew and so I gave in my notice at work. Those last weeks before my second summer break proved a painful time. My patients at the hospital became increasingly disturbed so that I had to help them work at their separation fears and at the same time face my own. There were moments when it seemed to be a struggle without end. Nonetheless, I recognized how much stronger we all were: they, and I myself as well. Some of them were leaving now, at the same time as myself. One or two of them had been quite psychotic when they came, almost stupefied with drugs previous doctors had prescribed. Now, three or four years later, they were taking more and more responsibility for their actions and their lives. Thinking about these results I felt encouraged and more confident.

The more that I began to think about my patients' future lives, the more humble I became. For I had to recognize with what minimal support some of them were setting out to build where mainly ruins marked earlier attempts at life. And some of them were doing this with a confidence and trust that our Unit had instilled and which my own therapeutic work had contributed towards. I could think along these lines of slowly growing self-respect because I felt much less afraid of interpreting it as arrogance and pride, or that magic was at work: the magic that the schizoid mind resorts to out of sheer despair of making the ascent to health from that tangled underworld where every foothold seems to slip. Now I could clearly recognize that their progress was nothing of the sort, but the result of skill, concern and sheer hard work over many baffling years of two steps forward, one step back, as in my own case as well.

As my illness gradually yielded up such misconceptions a real belief in myself was slowly able to take root, replacing former arrogance with more genuine self-esteem. Why should I not be able to help other, future patients now, since this evidence was there?

'Alright,' I jibed, 'but work alone? Without a staff group's warm support?'

'You don't acknowledge what you are getting from me,' SK remarked. 'You still cannot acknowledge it for fear that you have emptied me.'

He was absolutely right. I looked into my inner world whose panorama had become increasingly familiar, and saw the empty, shrivelled shell of my 'mother' analyst the very instant I confessed to how much help I had received.

'You don't believe,' SK went on, 'that I can replenish myself. That everything I give to you is given very willingly. The summer break you see as meaning my collapse. You do not see the summer break as being trusted to maintain yourself and deal with your own anxieties.'

'I think I am beginning to,' I said a little shakily. 'But I feel terribly bereft now that I've left the hospital.'

'You seem to see it as a support,' came the cryptic reply.

'Doesn't everyone?' I asked more than a little bit amazed, 'see employment in that way?'

'You feel you can't support yourself. You feel empty inside yourself because you can't keep me inside.'

'Even now,' I sighed, 'that's true.'

'You don't think it will ever change.'

'I think I know it will because so many other things have

changed for the better,' I replied.

And on that note we said good-bye and parted for the summer break. It was for the second time.

During the four weeks apart I tried to see it as a trust. I struggled with the miseries that kept on engulfing me in the summery countryside where friends had lent us their old house which I knew and loved so much. But still the feeling flooded back that I had now lost everything: my nice job at the hospital and my analyst as well. I fought and struggled with my doubts, my rages in my inner world, but my cold, stiff fingers lost that life-raft time and time again, in lonely days and sleepless nights. Nonetheless, to my relief, the cardiac symptoms stayed away and that gave rise to bursts of hope.

The third autumn term began on a very dubious note. Where would I get patients from? Two supervision patients were still in treatment, that was true, but otherwise my diary showed little more than empty blanks. And yet I gradually felt unprecedented confidence as J kept saying: 'Look how long I sometimes have to wait for sales.' Once I myself had given up that reassuring monthly cheque, I started to appreciate J's inner stamina and calm, his belief in what he did, whether recognition came or an overdraft. I realized I had never once given this sufficient thought and felt considerably ashamed of my failure to have grasped this basic, existential fact. Now I saw how J had kept all those worries to himself. Never once had he complained or passed his personal self-doubts on, the way that I kept doing now.

But hardly had I settled down to what might have proved a lengthy wait, when referrals came along. And gradually I learned to live with the various ups and downs that private psycho-therapeutic work must invariably bring. Unpredictability is the troubled person's stamp. Every psychoanalyst finds patients who slam out on him. Sometimes one takes cases on all too painfully aware that they may not stay the course. For psychotherapy implies considerable frustrations felt most painfully around the start. How can it come naturally to discover clamorous needs only to find that they will not be directly gratified? How words can seem to come between the patient and the therapist till it is slowly understood that words *can* be a vehicle for communicating pain or fears that seem unspeakable.

Throughout the third year, gradually, the separation from SK went forward very stealthily. But while one part of me worked hard and well at the analysis, another part did all it could to undermine the task in hand. Session by session, month by month, I could hardly keep awake.

'You're half asleep,' SK would say and keep repeating patiently.

At first I hardly questioned it. He might just as well have said: 'The blood is running through your veins.' It was, in fact, my usual state.

I had always gone to bed for 'a little sleep', or 'rest', at every opportunity, skedaddling from a dangerous world. Even in my social life, I slowly came to understand that I had tended to withdraw and dream whole evenings away while going through the motions of being present and alert. The minute that I could not be the centre of attention I would simply start to wander off into my favourite fantasies in which I was the only child and nobody could come between some perfect mother and myself.

This 'perfect' mother wanted me, and only me, all to herself. She would never let me go because she loved me much too much. I was her baby at the breast, her 'inside' baby for always, for an eternity of bliss. And now if SK wanted me to separate and stand alone, he could not love me. That was that. Time to fall asleep and dream my consoling fantasy, dead to the world. To go and die.

This syndrome also has a name. It is to feel 'depersonalized'. To be a person simply seems much too much like sheer hard work. It is also dangerous. A person tends to be attacked, so the deeper terrors run. A person often makes mistakes. A person feels and suffers pain, a person loves, who dare not love. A person has all sorts of needs and cannot remain an isolate. A person feels at risk, exposed. A person is supposed to take full responsibility. In any case, a person grows and that, to me, meant grows apart from her psychoanalyst. Oh no. It simply wasn't on. Be separate? Not at any price, my schizophrenic illness sang and tried to rock me back to sleep. At times it seemed beyond a joke. And still I struggled in the coils of this fateful lullaby.

Then, slowly, slowly, I woke up. My routine bedtime slowly moved from eight to nine, to ten o'clock, then to eleven in due course. Even midnight was no more a sheer impossibility. I felt more lively and began to feel entitled to make plans. In the third summer break I flew to California all alone. True, I was to stay with friends. I still had to be 'taken in', because I felt unable to make real provision for myself. But nonetheless, I made the move. After a few days on the coast, strangled by the sickly fog that devastates Los Angeles, I crossed the desert in a Greyhound bus to Taos, in New Mexico. I had always wanted to visit Lawrence's old ranch, and some friends had an adobe house six or seven miles away. I spent a joyful, carefree week in that clear and sparkling air, awestruck by the starry nights, the deep red mountains in the setting sun, the gorges of the Rio Grande, an eternity removed from the mute, industrial sprawl.

I knew this wellbeing was still horribly precarious, that it was conditional on hospitality and warmth to a maddening degree, that it could easily collapse if I was shown indifference or slighted in some trivial way. But it just so happened that I was not, and therefore the fourth year began on a much more hopeful note.

After this holiday I knew that I could keep SK 'inside' considerably more easily. Slowly I began to feel how to differentiate between having him inside as a protection and a good, and getting rid of him again with the old hostility. In other words, I had to learn, late in my own adult life, what babies and small children may learn quite automatically where everything goes well enough in the first years of their life.

By the fifth year I had grasped that this was what it was about in the most simplistic terms. But if I felt more separate now, I also felt much more at risk from almost every kind of harm and danger in realistic terms. These I had previously denied, when I had gone about my life padded in omnipotence. But as it cracked, this reinforced the armour of this crude defence. Once again I seemed to feel that I could handle anything and every contingency and went about my daily life like a very bloated frog.

Then, one day, I had a dream. I took a room in a hotel that was splendid beyond words. Inside that room there stood a car, seemingly rented for my stay. It was a most alluring car, such as I had sometimes seen streaking up the motorway: a flash of silver and a gleam of steel, so very powerful and fast it seemed to breathe a trail of fire from two powerful exhausts. But when I tried to start it up, where it stood ready by my bed to take me anywhere at all, it spluttered and refused to start. Waiters and bellboys had to come and tinker with it while I watched their efforts strangely unperturbed. But in the dream it failed to start.

'That car is your omnipotence,' SK pointed out to me.

I could see it instantly. And as I watched in dismay, a gaseous bubble seemed to burst and turn into a parachute in which I hurtled down through space, wondering if there was an earth ready to catch me when I came. For several days on end I fell, horribly afraid and also very much ashamed of all my grandiosity with its incidental proof of how very readily I still devalued the good help my analyst kept offering me. Now I saw clearly how it had mainly defended me against a sense of utter helplessness once I found that I could not control his movements totally. But now that I felt stronger and more self-reliant, it had served some of its purpose, anyway.

The earth was waiting, in the end, when my feet at last touched ground. But for many months to come I walked it feeling very strange. The ground felt dangerous and rough. The wind blew cold into my face and every sort of danger lurked from which I had quite clearly claimed divine immunity before. Giving up omnipotence, even to a small degree, proved to be a humbling task. But as with every other change that embraced reality it soon brought countless benefits. Once I was walking on the ground instead of floating on air, the fear of falling grew much less: the old, old fear of being dropped. And having landed on the earth, instead of hovering in space, I could slowly start to move into my actual body more, from which a sense of balance grew that I had not enjoyed before, but had always suffered from a fear of falling, even from a chair.

On the other hand I now had to face realistic dangers that I had previously denied, which then appeared the best way out. Where I had intervened in brawls of outsize drunkards in the dark and drizzle of a weekend night, I skirted these occasions now. And having learnt at last to trust my analyst implicitly, like a trusting little child that has never been let down, I had to learn the hard way that the world at large can bite and needs a circumspect approach. But such precautions are, of course, very different in kind from the suspicious overtones and constant brooding upon slights and wrongs that are the schizophrenic norm, forbidding any peace of mind or genuine relationships. Nevertheless, all progress came in these crude, unwieldy forms that required whittling down until they were amenable and could be handled easily in the complex everyday as ordinary social skills.

In this manner life became a more familiar machine. Its endless tricks became subdued. Instead of always conking out, like some accident-prone car, a dud off the production line, it tended, on the contrary, to exemplary displays of day-to-day benevolence. While the actual cars I owned, inevitably followed suit. Nasty bangers were replaced by something more reliable. And finally I ended with an automatic Volvo with power-steering: massive, safe, a great protective shell of steel around me on the daily road: a symbol of solidity. 'Keep your valuables safe,' the advertisement had read. And what I valued most of all were those who travelled in my car which now extended to myself in a realistic way. I was no longer so much trash in my own, uncertain eyes. I knew that patients, family and friends all wanted me to stay around as long as it was possible, because they loved me and I played a worthwhile part in all their lives. I had been quite devoid of this reassurance at the start when I had felt like so much foam bobbing on an empty sea.

But even now, in the fifth year, my fires of ever-present hate were still burning very bright. At best the flames would die away to embers, only to leap back to murderous hostility when holidays obliged me to share my precious analyst. When I was not the only one and so felt slighted, overlooked, some infant part of me still launched into an all-out attack of scorched earth policy, annihilating everything, including above all my 'internal' analyst.

In the wake of this mechanism came constant hypochondria. I felt convinced that there must be something that was very bad and so dangerous inside that I refused to take a look at what exactly it might be. The risk involved seemed much too great. The thing itself might eat me up. There was no knowing, ran my fears, what monster I was up against. Then, slowly, as those fears grew less and I confronted them at last, I found a devilish machine like a waste-disposal unit built into certain kitchen sinks. It ground up everything that failed to pacify me instantly, and threw it out as so much slush.

As I lay there on the couch I could watch it go to work the very minute that I felt angry with my analyst. One, two, three and out he went, when I would be at risk again from all the old, fragmented ills, growling suspicions and alarms, or sirens wailing in the night, predicting instantaneous death. Because, in inner fantasies, my psychoanalyst-turned-slush inside me would retaliate inside my kidneys, bowls or womb or any other hiding place, causing symptoms of all kinds, while the 'good' internal one was no longer in his place to keep me safe from fear and harm. How would this be resolved? But, as was generally the case with every new phenomenon, when I began to study it for an honest length of time sufficiently unflinchingly, however frightful it might seem, it agreed spontaneously to let itself be modified.

I still recall the Sunday when that great, cumbersome machine said: 'Look, I am redundant now.'

'But if you go,' I said in fear, 'what will take up all the space that you have occupied till now?'

'You will see,' came the reply.

How was it going to get out, I quavered quite uneasily. Having babies was one thing, but this seemed many times more large and made of concrete and of steel. What opening did the body have to rid itself of such machines? Yet, within minutes, it was gone. Nor did it leave an empty hole or some frightful, gaping gash. Good feelings and self-confidence quickly flowed into the space those angry teeth had occupied. But another problem was already waiting in the wings, quite as bitter and as sad as any of the previous ones. It was a case of genuine guilt about the daughters I had left and the tragic death of S. In the past these tragedies were merely part and parcel of the omnipotent responsibility I felt for each and everyone. If every single pain and grief in the whole, wide world could be attributed to me then I was also innocent of personal offence and lapse, so that the resulting pain could not get me in its grip. I was, of course, perpetually in some sort of muddled grief over this or that quite vague and distant happening and felt extremely virtuous to be so soft-hearted and kind. Whereas in reality all this was day-dream sentiment in some land of make-believe.

But now that this omnipotence had been gradually reduced, and the hostility and hate that were also, in the past, often aimed against myself, had been somewhat modified, these changes left me strong enough to confront the actual pain belonging to my personal life. And since I had discovered how enriched a life can be once we grow strong enough to offer Life itself an open house, whatsoever it may bring, by the same token I now knew the scale of loss where literal death, and all the forms of living death, confiscate this priceless gift. The certain knowledge that I had, in three separate instances, contributed towards that loss, which, in one case certainly, could not ever be made good – had to be confronted now.

When my analysis began my 'inner' world was occupied by 'dead inner objects', as we say. My 'inner' mother had been dead, father, brother, everyone. I was some sort of burial ground of the generations, as long as my destructiveness was felt to be omnipotent. Through five analytic years I began to question this. Gradually, as my belief in my loving feelings grew and brought the hope that I might repair the damage I caused from day to day in anger and hostility, these 'inner dead' stirred back to life; the mausoleum yielded up its former contents in as far as reality allowed. Now this space within myself had to be allocated to my loved ones who were *really* dead, or suffering in reality. Until this time they had shared a shadowy mass grave since I had not mourned them individually because I did not have the strength. And so this mourning now began.

Meanwhile, on the joyful side, others were restored to me whom I had long since given up. As usual this process was initiated by a dream. In it I was drying up for some friends after a party, when suddenly a pretty jug of Victorian design broke in two within my hands. I was about to throw it out when my friends said all at once: 'No, you can mend it easily.' And I recalled that there existed a glue which the experts always used. On the following night I dreamt that I was to meet someone outside a house in Holland Park. The street was one I dearly loved. Judging by its ambience, the house must formerly have been a beautiful, substantial home. But when I described it to SK I hesitated, and then said it looked like a psychotic house. A matted tangle of dark trees obscured the steps to the front door. The steps themselves were cluttered with fragmented statues, picture frames, a sort of jumbled overspill of what, at one time, must have been an exuberant, creative family. But the front door, I could see, was vandalized and boarded up. I rang the bell but did not expect anybody to appear. After some moments, nonetheless, an old, half-crazy woman did mysteriously materialize, perhaps from the basement steps. She made me think of someone whom I had once loved very much. I hoped I would remember whom. I then went on to speak about a recent evening with friends in their little attic flat which was in that very road. I said the sunset that evening had been exceptionally marvellous seen from their window so high up, then added that none of this seemed to take me anywhere.

'It sounds,' said SK, 'rather like a baby at the breast looking down at mother's beautiful body.'

Deeply moved I said it did and that the whole dream now made sense. For I had at last reached back to the mother I once loved who was now securely linked with the dark, psychotic house, from whose interior nonetheless a mother answered my call whenever I had rung the bell; even if she had not been the perfect mother that my wilfulness had felt itself entitled to.

Where does all this leave me now? Very, very different from anything I had conceived at the outset of this marathon. I had imagined I would be fearless, glamorous and strong like the Valkyrie of the myth or like the alluring masterpiece concocted in those Suffolk years.

A woman who is fifty-five meets my steady, searching gaze. A woman who might very well have been a grandmother by now if only, many years ago, she had been able to be a mother in the deepest sense. She has forgiven herself now for many failings of the past and feels a sense of gratitude that although her grandmother tragically killed herself so that her mother could not help but flounder in all sorts of ways, she herself was mended late but not too late by any means.

That our children may become our victims inadvertently is a sorrow we must bear. Yet once they reach adulthood how they resolve this legacy is a matter for themselves. However much I long for it I must accept that they may not at all follow the path which carried me through a full analysis.

B was on the other hand rescued from an orphan's fate, and D seems safely on the way to becoming a steady man, blessed with many first-rate gifts, and above all with the capacity to utilize them joyfully, enriching family and friends. The masterpiece had

gradually melted down to *terra firma*, to the reality of psycho-therapist and wife. A wife who can feel gratitude that J could keep such love alive through many thankless, tragic years to be rewarded by a true companion in the very end, such as he would have well deserved much sooner in an ideal world. That ideal world we do not have, which is not to say that we may not work towards it doggedly out of the necessity of our deepest hopes and love; for work is neither more nor less than these two blessings actualized. It is one of the reasons why work may never be denied to anyone, at any time.

Such work is the expression of our true endowments and our natural gifts, sharpened against the stones we pass, to grow in their own special way. They may bear neither flower nor fruit if distorted by the drive of crass ambition and material gain, all of which are rooted in the attention-seeking of the child that feels it has been overlooked. True fruit or seed may often look strangely colourless, viewed through a prospector's eyes.

In psychotherapy I found my shoulder's small place on the wheel. As a child, in Switzerland, I was always awe-struck by the great St Bernard dogs who found the victims of an avalanche with certain basic sustenance in a basket round their necks. Now, day by day I sit and watch frozen people come to life. How do I view this offering in psychoanalytic terms: in terms of my own new-found life?

Onto that awesome stage of Freud, Melanie Klein brought little wooden toys. My great nursery in Berlin had a cupboard for our toys. The big shelves were out of reach. There was a key that Nanny kept. Most of the toys had cost so much, no one must play with them at all. They might get broken, God forbid.

There was a chauffeur, cook and maids, nannies and gardeners – an entourage – but no one in that stiff, cool world kept glue or putty, screws or nails – the wherewithal to make repairs. Broken meant finished, damaged, dead! The thing that frightens children most: it cannot be mended or put right: the madman's terrible despair from which all ugly secrets stem that cut man off from other men.

Melanie Klein had little drawers that even the smallest child could reach. They opened very easily and every child could have his own. The contents were for daily use. If they got broken, messed or spoilt, it was far from being the end. It was, the frightened children learnt, where the story could begin.

Impressive though my nursery was with its treasury of toys, in that sumptuous, stricken house that the dark ivy clambered round, I have enchanted playgrounds now with drawers that open, toys that mend and every shelf within my reach: where messes mostly get cleared up and scolding hardly matters much because I know that I am good, although quite often also bad.

In the beginning, there is love.

It makes the world a safer place. It means we do not have to hide.

It means we can come out to play with all the children everywhere, at home on earth and in ourselves.

Postscript

REFLECTIONS AFTER ONE DECADE

How much lifetime has passed. This book was actually written near enough half-way through a nine-year analysis. By the time it went to press I might already have composed something of a variation. I was, in part, a different person, which is always the case with the making of new growth. However, the original assuredly had caught a moment which I was not prepared to scuttle on account of younger shoots. 'If I cannot be myself in what I write, then my work would be nothing but lies and humbug';* and now that some four years have passed since I left that Kleinian Home in a row of London houses, at the foot of a small hill, I know that I must try to capture a fragment of truth again, while knowing that it too, in time, will again be superseded.

The last few months and final weeks of the analysis, continued five times a week to the hour of termination, had been punctuated by some deeply gratifying sessions of a profoundly peaceful nature, which perhaps is what is meant by bliss. We agreed that they felt like a satisfying feed, both for mother and for infant. Both were thriving, one could say. What Tustin† has evoked so well as 'a rhythm of safety' where the mouth and breast achieve harmonious co-operation after troubling trial and error, was gaining in ascendancy. After a life of daunting struggle it was becoming *safe to be*, as I believed with some conviction.

I was right and I was wrong. I was wrong in as far as it is not given us to know what spectres have remained in hiding from the analytic process – for the time being anyway, since by their nature

*Margaret I. Little, 'Winnicott working in areas where psychotic anxieties predominate', *Free Associations* 3, 1985.
†Frances, Tustin, *Autistic Barriers in Neurotic Patients*. Karnac Books, 1986.

they are legion. Much remains to be done in our self-analysis through the years that lie ahead until that final curtain falls. This is part of the norm. Every analysis, for all the work that is accomplished, only leads us to the place from which our self can now take over, even if in steadfast dialogue with our inner analyst. It may make us sad or angry; we may feel that we have been once again left in the lurch, until sooner, if not later, we rouse ourselves to the fact that we can take this function over, well equipped for the task, even if a baby-part digs its toes in now and then and would rather still be carried.

I knew that something was 'still wrong', some major issue unresolved, when my feelings for my mother reverted to a state of turmoil as the weeks and months slipped by. Determined not to be defeated, to soldier on, though on my own, I decided to make something of this latest set-back and research and write a book on the mother–daughter dyad from 8,000 BC, the time of the first artefacts.* Perhaps, I hoped, these excavations would lead to further food for thought, and so indeed it proved to be. The long-drawn out struggle with that task, over all of five years, was a most healing undertaking, a mysterious therapy. But by the end of its first year, while I was labouring to assemble 'The psychotic mother and her daughter', as that chapter is called, I fell quite seriously ill and recognized conversion symptons – psychological distress which manifests in body language.

What on earth was going on in those reaches of my mind to which I clearly still lacked access? A week before, I had returned to my Kleinian Home for that eventful interview known as a 'follow-up'. On the day, it seemed I had mainly good news to report; that, at least, was how I played it: the old, old need to 'reassure' my 'anxious mother-analyst'. Yes, it had been a happy year and also a rewarding one. After long preliminaries the book had recently appeared, and I had, of course, mailed the first available copy to my former analyst. I said the book was doing well.

'You would like me to say, perhaps, that I too am pleased with it?'

'Naturally,' came the reply, far too readily, 'but I know you will not say it.'

---

*Ten Thousand Years of Mother–Daughter. Free Association Books, 1989 (provisional title).

Denying a profound distress at these analytic tactics, belonging to my 'nursery years', I rationalized that my analyst's refusal stems from a rigorous school of thought that a patient has to learn to validate his own achievements without depending on a feed-back to a 'childish' extent. With this I warmly disagree and I recognize with hindsight that a deeper part of me interprets this as 'crazy talk'. Neither, at the time, was I capable of feeling these urgent misgivings, let alone speaking of them, 'spoiling' these precious moments with anger or 'disagreement'. Had I not lived for this reunion for all of fourteen homesick months?

I left considerably shaken after exactly fifty minutes! I knew that psychoanalysts tend to handle the occasion in very different ways; but this austerer version nearly broke my heart, so that it started getting up to its earlier tricks again, in due course with a vengeance. Looking inward I could see that there was a part of me which simply did not want to live under 'such circumstances'. What these circumstances were, I would have no inkling of for an unknown stretch of time, while I was bound to recognize that the death and life instincts seemed precariously defused by sheer narcissistic rage with its cold and hostile tantrums. These I was familiar with. What troubled me considerably was some new element to which I was still a stranger.

Meanwhile many serious questions on the theme of 'termination' raised themselves in my mind. These, as I have since discovered, occupy experienced colleagues and are far from resolved. This adult weaning constitutes one of life's major crises. A close friend of mine had died, within months of terminating, of a fulminating cancer which had suddenly appeared when she was in her early forties. Should weaning be more gradual, which is one point of view? Was I going to survive?

'It can sometimes take two years to really settle down after an analysis. Let's see how things are after Easter,' came the written reply to my very anxious letter. Easter was nine months away, but I felt comforted. While one part of me shrieked: 'Help, please help, this is crazy', another part held onto trust. I could go along with that. More than anything I wanted to make a real go of it after receiving so much help, after feeling so much stronger, more self-reliant and optimistic in one part of myself, despite the latest difficulties. After all, I was no stranger to the sheer cussedness of

149

mind. I knew about the ways of splitting. I knew that if we split our object we split our Ego, there and then. That this was happening I could tell. I also sensed that this was not just about hostility – about a 'good' and 'bad' mother. There was more to it than that and I would have to be patient, hoping to make sense of things in the goodness of time.

'You might *like* more analysis, but I do not think you *need* it.' This was how matters rested after the second interview. Again I had tended to make light of serious difficulties. Again I had not yet been ready to use the opportunity to come out into the open with recurring inner rages, to raise them in the here and now with my 'rejecting' analyst, who, I felt, still seemed determined to simply 'wash his hands of me'. In my childhood I had sometimes taken a perverse pleasure in attacking large anthills vigorously with a stick. I was perfectly aware, at that age of six or seven, that I was laying to waste, with considerable glee, a monument which represented years of laborious work. Was that what I was doing now with one part of myself to my good analysis? It was undoubtedly the case, but precisely for what reason?

Of course, in between the rages calmer weather returned, when SK was reinstated in the warmth of loving feelings, even though we were apart, or else, as I knew very well, I would have lapsed into psychosis. None the less, a review of *My Kleinian Home* in a psychoanalytic journal kept nagging in my mind, for it had been written by someone whose views I could respect: that the transference I described to my Kleinian analyst seemed highly idealized.

I thought about it carefully and decided it was true, certainly at the time of writing. But that had surely been resolved during the ensuing years? I pondered. I felt none too certain. An idealized transference is, as a working rule, a negative one in disguise, where primitive anxieties are still at work in the unconscious. This is quite a serious matter. What had I been playing at? Where had I fooled myself, always assuming that I had? What was being covered up? The 'syndrome' of conversion symptons was quite disabling at times. There were days I felt too frightened to cross a busy road alone. As for long-distance driving, after forty blameless years, I felt convinced that I was a ruthless danger on the roads. A journey of ten or twenty miles proved an edurance test of terrifying proportions, yet in the past I used to cross France happily in two days. I felt angry and perplexed and knew moments of despair, of abject hopelessness, but drew comfort from the fact that a much admired colleague admitted in a heart to heart to a very similar experience from which she had gradually made a complete recovery. Were patients who had suffered from major autistic difficulties perhaps particularly prone to such life-shaking reactions to the end of an analysis? It seemed quite likely, we agreed, during a summer day of very fruitful discussions. I had to stay overnight, quite unable to face a drive of twenty miles back home. I knew that something was amiss in my relationship to my 'inner' analyst. But had not SK taught me how to wait in the dark, cheerfully, with optimism, since this represents one side of the creative process, the other side of that coin: the light of human understanding?

The answer, as so often, came from psychotherapeutic work in progress with certain patients who had known the life-disrupting hazards of having a psychotic mother. By 'psychotic' I do not mean 'insane' in the accepted sense, though some of those mothers, without a doubt, fell into that category, intermittently at least. I mean 'psychotic' in the sense in which Bion has defined it – that every personality consists of psychotic, neurotic and healthy parts which co-exist in all of us, but in various proportions, with variable ascendancies. The psychotic part is marked by intolerance to frustration which, with an excess of destructive impulses, leads to a violent hatred of reality, both internal and external. Such a hatred extends to all the aspects and organs of human consciousness in a futile attempt to escape from psychic pain, a dread of annihilation and of falling to bits.

Through the years I had grown increasingly aware that this poses mammoth problems for the infants of such mothers which are later on in life obstinately difficult to begin to sift and sort. 'Difficult', I mean, beyond much that is already known and written, as our understanding deepens, especially in the sphere of preverbal burdening.

Month by month and year by year I gradually became clearer that to try and help these patients to begin to free themselves from a baffling submission to their mothers' states of mind, as they tear into the infant psyche from earliest preverbal days when it is the softest putty, was an awe-inspiring task.

One morning one of these patients brought a certain dream. It concerned a psychotherapist of roughly my own age. Her associations were to a sad and lonely spinster. After some exploration of the dream's parameters, none of which led to its heart, I said that it was interesting that she saw me in this manner, as such a poor spinster-mother. In the context of the whole there were reasons to believe that these distortions belonged to notions other than envy. She burst out that she did *not* see me. Did not see me at all, which was the reason, she continued, with considerable feeling, why she could not take me in as a good, supporting person.

'Perhaps you are afraid,' I ventured, 'that if you saw me properly, you would see that I was crazy, as crazy as your mother was.'

'Yes, of course,' came the reply, with that matter-of-factness, where all had been obscure before, which can take one's breath away. 'She could put herself together, whenever there were visitors, just like you do for your patients, but the minute that they left that façade fell to pieces.' For all I know, you too are mad, was the obvious implication. How it echoed certain terrors of my own childhood years!

This patient had often asked to see inside my cupboards. Now it suddenly seemed clear: she needed to *see* and *know* what I did with my chaos. Where was I hiding it? Although she often displayed a very loving transference, if a little idealized, she also kept me, as we knew, at a treacherous distance. Now we knew one reason why: she was convinced that I was mad; that any day my façade was bound, for sure, to crack wide open and reveal that spectre which had ransacked her childhood years of deep security or meaning, as it had ransacked mine.

What do I mean by this 'spectre' which had not materialized in my own analysis as a totality with that utter conviction it was now assuming as my patient and I began to face the daunting task of confronting it together?

It is a conglormeration, brewed of witch and demon, of volcanoes that erupt, mud and earthquakes that send down roaring landslides of sewage, of teeth in a distorted leer, of part-objects and phantoms daubed with our own sadism, which we spew up in response to experiencing an absence where there ought to be a mother, in every meaning of the sense, far beyond a mere presence. Here is the stuff of our worst nightmares, of a 'bad' LSD trip, the ogre who in pantomimes makes all the children scream, the Bad Fairy, or the murderer, strangler, rapist or intruder: a synthesis of such pure terror that words are almost bound to fail us. This miasma is, of course, coloured by our own projections, for all that it must contain intrinsic realities.

Furthermore, the phantom tends to occupy our mental space and leave very little room for therapeutic manoeuvre, often over many years. The term 'bad object' really fails to convey this distortion, which is incompatible with sufficient sanity. Any less afflicted parts of the personality are virtually crowded out to a thin periphery. The presence of this constellation, different in every case, rarely lets us rest by day or achieve peace of mind. Its continuous persecution can drive us to drink or crime, drug addiction, suicide and every form of acting out. Here defences like denial, omnipotence, splitting and projection all have their early foundation. Here, finally, fragmentation, with its mad Siren's song, promising a reprieve from this lurid visitation, lures us to that escape which will lead to the madhouse.

A good-enough mother *is* the ground of her infant's being for as long as required in his or her earliest making. No one would plant a rose in slabs of crumbling lava. The infant mind will sense acutely, and be set awash by terror, when a mother's mind is reeling, or is wildly out of kilter, the more so since it will be hijacked to serve as a container for maternal distress.

The actual terrors may, at first, be little different in kind, from those of any other infant when it is passing through what Mrs Klein has called, the 'paranoid-schizoid position'. But here reality-testing, instead of bringing to bear understanding and warmth to modify this dangerous turmoil, keeps reinforcing it. To take an unflinching look into the heart of the crater of this catastrophe takes heroic courage – the more so since the patient fears that, just like himself, the analyst 'cannot stand it', that he may up and run at the first hint of such material. For that very reason it will either remain hidden or only surface in disguise and so finely fragmented, that it may well be missed.

But the failure to begin to face this devastation of the psychotic parts of the personality is also the patient's failure, as it was in my own case. For years on end I remained 'half-asleep' in my sessions and withdrew into retreat rather than confront these issues. I clung to the precarious life-rafts of my existing sanity. Had they not carried me afloat on the stormy inner seas of my life experience, and kept my head above water, even if precariously?

If my fingers were to slip, who was going to guarantee that I was not swept away, never to be seen again in the land of the living outside mental institutions? To risk this final letting go, and throw my terrified arms around my analyst with total trust and commitment, was an act of fortitude which throughout those years I was never – quite – able to make. I believed that I had done it. None the less some part of me had been clearly hanging back until that session with my patient.

As we worked at it that morning and for weeks to come, SK was safely at my side, holding my inner hand. I left that session with my patient feeling considerably healed. She herself, I knew, had taken that first essential step of confronting the spectre. We were both on the way, even if, as was only proper, I was ahead of her. We would both be home and dry in the goodness of time, both of us safely held by the analytic process where it flows clean and bright, like a clear mountain stream. I might have my difficulties, but I knew I was not mad. She was welcome to look, so to speak, in my cupboards, for at this time of my life I was able to contain my own areas of chaos well enough from day to day, above all while I worked.

While reflecting on these issues in some depth throughout the day, I was able to observe my idealized transference to my inner analyst give a funny little shudder and begin to dissolve. Hopefully, in time, it would become a thing of the past, as self-analysis continued. It had, as I could clearly see, been set up to protect me against this anxiety – a profound suspicion that my analyst was *mad*!

I could see in retrospect that even at the end of my analysis, I had still lacked the Ego strength to confront these lurid images of my earliest 'memories', deeply coloured as they are by our own phantasy-creations into an ultimate concoction which is nearer to a myth. It was I who had pressed to end the analysis, to have some life-time free of that taste of regression which the process must impose, inevitably to some degree. And SK had not objected, as he had in the past when such a proposition rested all too clearly on resistance: a cop-out in other words.

Some patients have, we know, to stop just when they are on the brink of some pain they cannot face, some issue that their defences are not up to dealing with at this time in their life. Often they must remain the best and final judge of that, provided what has been accomplished seems substantial enough, in terms of having got to grips with earliest anxieties, to offer reasonable prospects of future stability. So I had to slog it out as part of that later process of self-analysis, this matter of his 'crazy talk' which had 'confirmed' my old suspicions, deep in hiding all along.

My mother tended to ignore me, as I had experienced it. She had failed to 'recognize' me in that deepest personal sense from which our truest selfhood springs: our right to separate existence, of honest contact and free choice. Like a ship in the night, she had somehow passed me by, this secretive and stubborn daughter, with her wild, unruly ways, with her flying aspirations and rich imaginative life with its alarming excesses. Is it not high time we acknowledged areas of child abuse, every bit as catastrophic as the physical ones currently in every headline, which children are subjected to when the primary care-takers are unsteady and awash? Are there not children who are pushed to murder their soul each day, to tear it out by the roots, or submit to bestial penetration of the most private parts of their unfolding psyche, if any portion shall survive, in that situation of abject dependency? Could I really, really trust that SK was different?

During that morning session everything fell into place. My analyst was not mad! It was safe for me *to be* in the place where I had sprung from the good ground of his being. Just as with the rest of us, his personality must have its own share of difficulties, 'the Shadow', as the Jungians say. Besides, to some degree these fuel all creativity, whether it is in the arts, the craft of the analyst, or the poetry we weave into our every day.

I was now in a position to take this matter up with some of my other patients, as it appeared in new material linked to a backlog from the past. It seemed a universal rule. Where a mother was disturbed, bordering on the psychotic, or even manifestly so, I, the therapist, was not to be trusted for a moment. I was crazy. I was mad and every inconsistency, every sign of inner muddle, fatigue or change of tone of voice, was the thin end of the wedge. These patients, who, like myself, had devoted a childhood to a continuous struggle in forlorn attempts to keep maternal chaos at bay, had, before they could get better, to reach back to the hells of that teetering mode of being. A mode where they monitor the therapist's states of mind with such acute anxiety that there is little time left over to start to think about themselves.

Formerly, what was the point? As their mother's keeper, they were not entitled to an existence of their own. How could they take an hour off to concentrate on their studies or any aspect of their life, even if this slavery, which is painfully compulsive, engendered a murderous hatred which had, of course, to be denied?

I used to rage at my mother that she had engaged a nanny, while she travelled the big world, first of all with my father and later with her woman friend. I have clearly realized since that I owe to my Nanny every shred of sanity that had somehow kept me going, by the skin of my teeth, until my last analysis. It meant, as I came to see, that my feminine identification with good mother figures, was almost entirely with servants, with the obvious limitations and distortions this implies. It is only as a writer that I could identify with my actual 'good' mother, for in those Bavarian years she began to study folklore. She began to do research, and produced many papers which continue to appear with professional acclaim. Now, in her mid-eighties, she is still at this task. She begins to write in bed from five o'clock in the morning, and still visits the great libraries when the weather is kind.

In her personal life a willingness to help us all, children and grandchildren alike, to her best ability, is tremendously touching. When it comes to say good-bye, she can do so in the knowledge that she will be sadly missed and remembered with affection which she has amply earned these last decades of her life. Indeed, this exemplary autumn she won for herself is a hard act to follow. It is my hope that I may still have that opportunity.

We enter analysis or psychotherapy, basically, as an infant, regardless of our actual age. To enter, as I did, at fifty, meant, I found, that I emerged as an old age pensioner according to our social institutions. While it seemed rather nice to collect a free travel pass, it was daunting and painful to feel that my life had just begun, in the best and fullest meaning, so soon before closing time. But perhaps, in one sense, that is always the case. Our life is, so to speak, on loan from one moment to the next. We need to spend it in that light to our best ability.

Meanwhile J and I can share a prolonged Indian summer in the workshops of our London home. I had never liked the district, and the house lacked a garden, which the studio occupies. For years we hunted for a home with a studio *and* a garden we might be able to afford. Then, one day, the house next door suddenly whent up for sale. A somewhat grotty boarding house, some of whose sounds and smells were rather less than edifying, we managed to acquire it with some help from my mother. A dream had finally come true. After almost three decades we now have a small, walled garden: access to the earth and sky. Our old gardener in Suffolk would, I think, be proud of me, although I very often long for a word of his advice.

J, at seventy-seven, grows younger every day. He still starts work at four a.m. as on our first night together, over three decades ago, so that by lunch-time he has covered an entire working day, seven days of the week. To be privy to the ways a blank canvas is transformed into glowing images, to a production line which he feels has begun, finally, to represent the truest statement of his heart, almost to his satisfaction, is a joy beyond belief. An earthly privilege, it seems almost an unearthly one.

Across the garden from the studio, but overlooking it, is my own writing room, and adjoining it the one to which I go to see my patients. J can hear my typewriter and I can hear the little hammer when he knocks up a frame. Here, in the Inner City, an oasis of great peace.

The Inner City prowls and growls all around us, day and night. Only recently I woke to find a young Black in my room. As I stirred, he disappeared over the garden wall as the first light of day was breaking. The car windows have been smashed and the tyres slashed with knives. I see all this as Civil War across the surface of our patient earth. That there is no need for it, is, of course, the saddest thing, for it is about privilege and majority exclusion.

Through our black, adopted daughter we have learnt once again what we already knew who both arrived on these shores as Jewish refugees: the savage horrors and disgrace of all racial persecution. This lovely girl, like all her friends, has had to face experiences we would have dearly liked to spare them.

In her girl-bedroom hangs, among the various pop-star posters, a painting J did of his father, seated at his cobbler's bench. She knows this grandfather died with the entire family when Hitler's henchmen sent the Warsaw Ghetto up in flames. Her own identification is largely with her own people, which in that sense is with ourselves, and so her life is taking off, the last one to fly the nest, in its own, true directions rooted in an impressive self. She has chosen to become a beauty therapist. 'Not an ugly one like us', said a colleague of mine smiling.

Are we ugly therapists? We inflict so much pain, as our patients may protest in the early days of treatment. That we are helping them, slowly to grow strong enough to experience the pain of the human condition, reflected in the outer world, as we, sadly, pillage it, will take them time to discover, as with the understanding that we can only feel joy deeply where we keep a home for pain – for both are finally 'suffered' just as Bion taught.

If in this autumn of our life the garden glows with seasonal flowers, we are grateful to enjoy such a blessed interlude.

D's birth had symbolised for me that a time of utter darkness was yielding to new light. He became my Messiah. He was hope personified, a dangerous throne for any baby whose priority must be to hear the drum of his heart calling him away – to life. I know that my earlier idealization spun a web of candy-floss which made that going somewhat sticky for both of us for a while, until my analysis began to sluice nice, clean water, just in the nick of time. The memory of that trap, its dangerous entanglement, sometimes still makes me fight shy and hold rather too far back in expression of my love just in case it overflows all those carefully built banks whose guardian I must be for life. He is now a married man, with a family of his own. Yes, I have a granddaughter who is now one year old – the sweetest gift we may receive at this hour of our life.

When she was all of five months old her mother left her in my care for a matter of two hours – the baby's first experience of no breast-on-demand! If I sensed what lay ahead, nothing had quite prepared me for the cataclysms we must share when that all-powerful assumption of mother-as-a-part-of-me received its first stupendous crack in her short life history.

She always had refused a bottle. As she sobbed and choked and drowned in the torrents of her tears, nothing I could do availed. The child I held close to me, as I paced her nursery floor, went cold and stiff in my arms. Her colour was a mottled grey. I dreaded that she might die between one gasp and the next. Her deprivation and distress occasioned me to bear witness to that homeostatic upset which underlies my wretched 'syndrome' when it chooses to appear, just as it underlies all psychosomatic illness at its primeval roots, even if the final form it takes is subsequently embroidered by later phantasies, where exposure to this rupture exceeds the resilience of an inborn constitution. At last, at last she fell asleep, still shaken by tremendous sobs at troubling interludes. Slowly, slowly colour crept back into those deathly cheeks, as they gradually grew warm once some inner thermostat had readjusted to life's flow.

Now she can spare her mother for a whole afternoon, provided everything goes well. But when Susie returns, I am bound to recognize that the baby in my care was really only half alive in the absence of her mother. Some part of her was hanging on, somehow making do with me, subsisting on our joint resources, until her source of life returns to the circle of their arms. It is such a humbling lesson to be this baby's 'second best'; to submit to that embargo at evolution's hands, how we can each be maimed if life carries mother off at the height of our needs and infant dependency.

During those months I used to pray: please, let nothing happen to the mother of this child. As an extension of that prayer, my anguish swept across the earth where war and man-made conflagration rip infants from their mothers' arms; where drought and famine take their toll on the heels of the mindless greed of the 'free democratic world', as we are pleased to call ourselves. I had to live through the extinction of this five-months-old child of my own flesh and blood, whom, I was unable to console, utterly helpless to revive, and shake with a deeper rage at what we are perpetrating in our arrogant white life-time.

Every joy has its price. Each even mobilizes certain memory traces in the computers of the mind. Had my own daughters not been torn from this same woman's arms? Was it not the same woman? I may not disown her now, but draw comfort from the fact that both these girls in their thirties, after painful travail, have picked up the scattered pieces to build them meaningful lives. With great generosity they do not hold the past against me, while I am well aware that in the depths of their hearts a lifelong sorrow comes and goes as inevitably as the tides of the travelling salty sea.

I am grateful in the knowledge that all my children have made use of psychotherapy, each according to their need, choosing from different schools and methods as they saw fit. I myself have equally moved on to explore many kinds of help on offer, with a growing interest. Classical analysis, as we know, ignores the body. Yet, as Freud always said, the Ego is a body-Ego. From my Alexander teacher I derived a fund of insights into how the body shrinks from its freedom like the mind; how it distorts its upright grace by the pull of anxious muscles. And I was deeply impressed by the way these teachers use themselves with such exquisite precision to untwist those in their care.

This gave me food for thought – how the intricate training of psychotherapists can lead to anxious inhibition in this particular sphere. As a training therapist I watch sadly how some students can insidiously be scared out of spontaneity, simple warmth and common sense, out of that direct response which springs from our humanness. How easily we forget that the concepts we are taught can only serve as scaffolding for our own observations and working creativity.

It is undoubtedly important that we do not undermine the serious and long-term task both parties, therapist and patient, are committed to. But the so-called 'blank screen', the notion that the therapist is supposed to represent – assuming it were possible – a cipher for the task in hand, introduces new distortions into a relationship whose effectiveness depends on the greatest inner freedom of a free-wheeling self on the part of the guide.

When this book of mine appeared almost four years ago, I was naturally concerned how my patients would respond if they should discover it, although I used my married name instead of my professional one. Inevitably, one by one, they tumbled to its existence, and I found no evidence, as I scanned the transference, that any of them came to harm from noxae thereby introduced.

A book has recently appeared with 20 random interviews of people who have undergone some form of psychotherapy.* Those who felt benefit from the experience without exception put it down to knowing that their therapist was a real and forthright person: a true and not a false self. Did not the greatest therapists – Freud, Klein, Winnicott and Frieda Fromm-Reichman, to mention only a few – according to testimony 'break the rules' in this respect, to their patients' benefit? How I myself drew heart from the occasional lapses of my Kleinian analyst into some minor confidence, brief discursion or aside.

This takes me to another aspect I have been reflecting on. A stance which is unnatural, beyond healthy discipline, as we relate to our work, might, in time, make us dislike it, with the insidious danger that we may dislike our patients by displacement on this ground. Nor am I happy in my mind about this category 'patient', as it sometimes surfaces from talk among practitioners. On occasion I detect a hint of dismissiveness or superiority which seems grossly out of place. We all have our difficulties: our psychopathology. None of us can say for certain that we may not succumb to a breakdown or to madness. Indeed, does not our daily work expose us to those very dangers to a notable degree? We labour under honest strain, sometimes very near the brink. Hopefully we learn our limits! Seriously disturbed patients, or areas of deep disturbance surfacing in every treatment that is well enough conducted, are bound to test our stamina, particularly at such times when our personal life has to meet another challenge. We are pupils throughout life even when they call us teachers.

None of this is to say that I hold with misconduct, with abuse of that power, which is virtually unparalleled, in this extraordinary encounter. But because this encounter in all its parentheses is itself the instrument which is designed to correct and over-ride the mutilations arising from the primary parent-child interface, there is no dispensation from crystalline openness – for all the courage this demands – provided this is not confused with crass exhibitionism or other forms of self-indulgence which we are obliged to sift and sort, time and again, in every session. Perhaps it helps if we select those whom we set out to help over such a span of

*Rosemary Dinnage, *One to One: Experience of Psychotherapy*. Viking Books, 1988.

our lifetime on the basis of some deeper liking; if we are clear in our own mind what catergories of difficulty we tend to feel uneasy with and where our best talents lie. No one can work against the grain, while all these matters finally will rest on slow experience.

It has also grown on me that only those individuals who know they have been deeply helped by their personal therapy have it in them to become healers in a vital sense; are able year by year to marshal the benevolence and clinical optimism to the task of guiding resurrection which remains the final aim.

Here I must remind myself that I am not writing a book on these fascinating themes, which shall instead remain the object of a future exercise. The same applies certainly to my ongoing explorations into body-therapies, for want of a better name for these important contributions. In the mental hospital where I worked for several years, we were fortunate to have active departments of art and music therapy. All of these have a place in the task of rehabilitation. Not everyone can make most use – can wring from the spoken word the very deepest resonance of symbol and imagination. I owe important insights to the lunch-time seminars with my colleagues, which we held every week to mutual edification. The longer life offers such opportunites of hindsight into my apprenticeship, the more I become aware how much I owe to so many, how inestimable were the riches I received through the years in the remaking of myself.

In asking me to add these pages, my publisher has given me a truly important present for which he has my gratitude, as indeed, for so much else. He has, I now appreciate as I come to the end, permitted me one more encounter with a hurt, impassioned child and a simultaneoous meeting, a heartfelt and serious one, with a half-familiar buoyant woman. She says she is a wife and mother of a grown family, a psychotherapist and writer, a bit of a gardner and cook. The day has barely begun, yet she sits here, at my desk, uses my old typewriter, smiles up at me and says: 'You know, we've come quite a way and not done badly in the end, all the awkward odds considered.'

We take a turn about the garden. 'Even that childhood,' she goes on, with an arm about my shoulder, 'what a double perspective it has slowly come to be. How many windows have opened, which were somehow closed before, to let the afternoon sun pour gold into the darkest corners.'

'You are right,' comes the reply. 'Despite the pain and difficulties, all the human limitations, vistas of obstinate strength slowly opened up to offer enormous opportunities so many are never given.'

'Make sure you take them all on board and continue to own them', come the now familiar words.

As these two beings, arm in arm, re-enter my working room through the sliding glass doors, they slowly merge into one: a deeply fortunate woman, who, to add to many others, also had the privilege of a good analysis at a time in her life when she could, at last, use it.

Of all the dreams we undergo is not the strangest of them all, the most mysterious and baffling, the undertaking of our life?

If I were asked today to explain the nature of the undoubted benefits of psychotherapy, where they are in evidence, I would say that we become more accessible to life; that the notion of defeat is replaced by a trust that our inner resources, harnessed to freed energies, will lead towards such achievements as sneaked into our dreams before; that where we died a thousand deaths, defeated by our hate and envy, our destructive impulses, we know that we can work our passage back to light and life again – in such lifetime as we own.

May 1988